The March to Corunna

The March to Corunna

Letters from Moore's Army in Portugal
and Spain during the Peninsular War
by a British Officer 1808-1809

Robert Ker Porter

LEONAUR

The March to Corunna
Letters from Moore's Army in Portugal
and Spain during the Peninsular War
by a British Officer 1808-1809
by Robert Ker Porter

First published under the title
Letters From
Portugal
and Spain

Leonaur is an imprint
of Oakpast Ltd

Copyright in this form © 2009 Oakpast Ltd

ISBN: 978-1-84677-924-4 (hardcover)
ISBN: 978-1-84677-923-7 (softcover)

http://www.leonaur.com

Publisher's Notes

Contents

Preface   7

Letters From Portugal and Spain   9

Preface

The following letters contain an account of the march and actions of the British army under Sir John Moore, from the day of their departure from Lisbon to that in which they embarked at Corunna.

They were written on the spot, and immediately as the events arose, of which they are the subjects. Hence the remarks they contain are totally independent of being influenced by after consequences; and are merely the observations of a man deeply interested in the scene before him.

As such they are offered to the public; a simple and authentic account of the disasters and blasted hopes of one of the finest armies, that ever left the British shore. It is narrated by a man who pretends to no better style than that learnt in camps: as a soldier he felt, as a soldier he writes; and to a soldier who bled in the fields of Spain he hopes his readers will grant their indulgence.

London, May, 1809.

Letters From Portugal and Spain

LETTER 1

Lisbon, September 30, 1808.

My Dear S———.

I address you first from this city, not having had an opportunity before of letting you know how I passed my time since we separated at Portsmouth.

You will remember how often I murmured at not being permitted to sail with Sir John Moore's army! However, as fate has ordered it, I have not to lament my hoped-for share in any victorious leaf added to their brows during that interval; as that expedition arrived too late to reap any part of Sir Arthur Wellesley's harvest of glory on the 21st of August. This month, so memorable in the annals of England, by numbering within its circle the proud days of Minden and of the Nile, now gems its calendar with that of Vimeira! a day indeed truly honourable to the commander who planned the battle, and to the brave men whose invincible steadiness rendered it victorious!

In proportion as I rejoiced in this triumph, the subsequent circumstances filled me with regret; and I was not at all astonished when I heard of the impression they have made in the British world. Newspapers brought out by a frigate just arrived, speak boldly in blaming the recent convention; and from officers lately come out, who were at Plymouth when the news was promulgated, I hear that the political electric shock it occasioned, lengthened the visages of all men. I may well say all, for it was not confined to our own countrymen; the woeful change shook even our allies; and the Portuguese stood staring at each other as if uncertain whether a mine or one of their old earthquakes had sprung under their feet. Much was expected from us.

Two great victories had already extended the laurels of Britain over the head of Lusitania. No impending blight appeared, to threaten a prevention of their spreading yet farther, even to overshadow with a thousand protecting arms, the whole people of this outraged country. These hopes are now blasted, and all is doubt and wonder. For us on this side the water to form a correct judgement on the subject is impossible. Ignorant of the motives which actuated our commanders to conclude the convention of Cintra, how can we decide on its cogency? There may be reasons behind the arras which we, who know not the secret springs of the council-chamber, may seek in vain. It behoves us, then, to be quiet, and await with patience the arrival of an explanation from England. You hold the keys of all our wonderments; and with the footsteps of knowledge, even at the distance of many a league, tread ground with ease, which, on the spot. We find a bewildering labyrinth.

You have promised to follow my pen with patience through all my continental wanderings! Should Spain be our future destination (which I hope in heaven may be the case, as I have a strong desire to visit that land, both of ancient and modern heroes), I will then promise you some amusement for the heavy task you have entailed upon yourself by my correspondence. Meanwhile, I shall not be idle in transmitting to your mental vision, an image of this capital; for itself and its vicinity present objects of ample interest to engage the attention of the curious observer,

You can form no idea of the magnificence of the view, on entering what is called the mouth of the Tagus. It ought rather to be considered an arm of the sea; so capacious is its breadth, so sublime the proud sweep of its waves. The shore on the Lisbon side is terminated by the bay of Cascars; on a point of which stands the Fort St. Julien, now occupied by our troops. This justly esteemed defence of the harbour is cut in the solid rock; it is therefore very irregular, but strong, and admirably adapted to its design. They say it was planned by the famous Don Sebastian, and executed under his eye. The country rises very high behind it; and though enriched here and there with a few orange and olive trees, owing to the season of the year the hills present a parched and arid appearance.

The banks of this celebrated river, the long-famed Tagus with golden islands, are spread with testimonies of its riches; villas, villages, and fortifications. On its bosom heave the proud fleets of Britain, intermixed with numbers of smaller vessels, whose lateen sails and copper-hued crews bring the, shores of the Nile, or of Barbary, before your awakened fancy, and produce a stretch of scene as splendid as romantic.

As our ships proceeded up the river, the land gradually advanced on either side; the suburbs of Lisbon appeared, and this commanding city rose in white majesty to the view of the admiring traveller.

Belem stands within a mile or two of Lisbon. Its approach is defended by a beautiful and. picturesque *pharos*, whose base is washed by the waves of the Tagus. This is doubtless, the work of some ancient Moorish artist, and exhibits no inconsiderable degree of proficiency in the arabesque taste. A vast chain, carved in stone, binds its angular form; and every ornament which decorates the walls is in harmony with the barbarous genius of the times. It is garrisoned; and though cannon have been planted there, no injury has been done by modern improvements to the Moorish beauties of the ancient edifice.

The convent at Belem is a building of the same character, but it has not fared so well. Its exterior has suffered both by time and absurd novelties; yet there is something in true grandeur which no art can destroy; and the majestic walls and rich ornaments of this venerable structure still strike the eye with admiration and respect.

Nearly opposite, on the adverse bank of the river, stands high and commanding, the romantic fort of St, Sebastian. It is well stored with cannon, and forms a strong barrier against any attack of the capital by sea.

On a nearer approach to Lisbon, it loses its parian hue; and on a closer investigation, the cleanliness which the external whiteness of the houses shining in the sun at a distance, leads one to expect, vanishes; and the miserably plastered dwellings present themselves in their true colours, bespattered with dirt of every description, and rendered almost intolerable by the accumulated filth, and the raging heat which draws their honours reaching up to heaven!

On disembarking I landed some distance from the suburbs. The foul imagination of Dean Swift himself could not prefigure the scene that presented itself: a chaos of nastiness, poverty, and wretchedness, lay on every side. Rags or nakedness seemed the condition of every person who approached me; except now and then, I saw a man enveloped in a mass of cloak, in no better state, hung in rented folds about him: leaving to the fancy to conceive the animated filth it concealed. In the midst of this squalid misery, the aspirings of vanity may still be seen in the immense cocked hats, which are enthusiastically prized and worn by old and young of every trade and description.—Masons, blacksmiths, muleteers, and barbers, while executing the duties of their calling, all possess this prodigious covering placed square to the front on their respective heads. Bonneted like ancient Pistol they look in garments like the tatterdemalions of our St. Giles's, or, when wrapped in their looped and ragged cloaks, appear so many Mad Toms burst from their keepers. This convenient *toga* is not confined to the men; both sexes use it, and wear it summer and winter, to exclude the heat in the one season, and the cold in the other.

While I gazed around at this strange assembly of dingy complexions, in more dingy *habiliments*, my curiosity had a new subject of surprise in the numberless rows of aloes which lined the road. The long-anticipated moment, which in England occurs only once in a hundred years, to see the aloe bloom and blow, is here enjoyed at every step. Farther in the country, I am told that hedges of aloes are as common as quick-set are with us. Their green bosoms were a pleasant relief to my eye from the augean sights that surrounded me; more disgusting, perhaps, to one who had so recently left the comforts and cleanliness of Great Britain.

While I am on this delectable subject (for as it first strikes the senses on entering Lisbon, it must, perforce, be the first noticed), I cannot but remark, that a nocturnal custom, once the stigma of Edinburgh, is most religiously observed in this ever-steaming capital. As soon as night casts her sable mantle over the city, the inhabitants collect their libations, and pour them out in rich potations upon the earth beneath. In fact, few seconds pass without the foot passenger being saluted, or most probably marked, by a *jet d'eau,* or something worse from the

teeming windows of the houses. Should the unlucky perambu-
lator chance to be within reach of the torrent, I fear he would
emerge with other ornaments hanging to his dress, than the
spangling globules of clear water. A brother officer of mine is so
afraid of these green and yellow cascades, that he never walks
to his quarters at night, without bearing above him the friendly
shield of an umbrella.

The French, when they were here, with all their vigilance,
could not put a stop to this abominable custom: every expedient was tried, but in vain; at last an order was issued, obliging
every domestic, or other person preparing the fall, to call out
three times "water comes!" before he emptied the utensil. But
nine times out of ten they omitted the warning until the launch
was made.

At present, the police is so weak and ill-managed, and the people so indolent and innately nasty, that no manual exertions are
made to remove the growing pestilence. They wait until the
hand of heaven saves them the trouble; the rainy season never
failing, by the torrents from the hills, to prove a good scavenger.
Indeed, when I look around me, and see the indignities cast
on our good mother earth, I am not surprised that she should
sometimes, in a fit of resentment, open her ponderous and marble jaws to engulf the whole mass, and take a mighty vengeance
on her insulters.

On my arrival, I found Lisbon fully garrisoned by our troops,
as was the castle, and all the forts along the river. General Beresford was the military governor; and the head-quarters of our
army were at Benefecca, about four miles from hence.

No pen can describe the delight of these oppressed people on
finding themselves released from so insatiable an enemy as the
French. In proportion as they saw occasions to appreciate their
deliverance, their hatred of the invaders augmented, and no
bounds could be put to their threats of revenge. If perchance an
unfortunate remnant of their late rulers remained behind, and
was found by any of the Portuguese, a stiletto was sure to find
its way to his heart. Indeed, so difficult was it to keep the spirit
of vengeance from breaking forth on the last division of the
French, that British escorts were obliged to guard them from
insults. I need only give you one instance, out of many, of this
determined hatred.

The frigate in which General Kellerman and his suite had embarked sprung her bow-sprit, and was obliged to put back. During her stay to refit, this well-known hero was imprudent enough to trust himself ashore; and being recognised by some Spanish officers, he was instantly attacked by the populace. Had he not been near the water, he must certainly have then paid with his life the forfeit of his extortions. Some of our men happened to be present; and after receiving several severe blows, he fell into the boat: our brave soldiers leaped in with him, and warding off the strokes of his justly enraged enemies, they rowed away, and left him in security. This gentleman, whose gallantry at the battle of Marengo is so well known, appears to have reversed the old motto of knighthood: *the glory, not the prey!* and brave as he certainly was, he seems to have given up the sole empire of his mind to the most insatiable avarice. When the town of Elvas was taken and sacked by his brethren in arms, he was heard to express his regret at not commanding the exploit, adding, "Next to Lisbon, it was the place best worth plundering!"

And the issue shewed, that he must have had much experience in the ravaging trade to have been so good a judge. The accumulation of property drawn from that unhappy city not only filled all the extra apartments in the hotels occupied by this horde of destroyers, but the house of the British factory was fated to be the receptacle of stolen goods: plate, books, indigo, cotton, everything that was moveable, was crammed up in this, perverted dwelling.

According to the recent convention, most of these articles would have been embarked for France as French property; but the public spirit and vigilance of our military governor, and the committee appointed by him, saved to the inhabitants of Lisbon upwards of two hundred thousand pounds value of private and public wealth. The latter being in church pictures, massive silver candalabrums, vases, &c, whose fashions and uses gave the lie to the French that they never had belonged to Portugal, shewed themselves as so many proofs of their plunder and falsehood.

This wise investigation of General Beresford proved to the inhabitants that we were not really (what, on the first publishing the terms of the convention, they had imagined), "the sanctioners of robbery, the protectors of plunderers, and the carriers of violated property."

When the general exultation at being delivered from the tyranny of Junot had subsided, the enthusiasm of the Portuguese gave way to thoughts of futurity; and the articles of the Cintra arrangement were canvassed. But one opinion prevailed. It checked the animated glow of triumph, and in its stead spread over the countenance the sickly paleness of discontent and suspicion. Seeing this, we cannot but turn our eyes to our neighbours in Spain, and think what they will say when they hear that the ships of their protectors and friends pour into almost the very bosom of their country, a body of their enemies, armed, well appointed, and untrammelled?

General Junot seemed to consider this convention in so favourable a light that, I am told, when he was taking leave of the owner of the house in which he had been quartered, "Sir (said he to him), I shall return hither in the course of a few months; and as this house is my property, I request you will look out for another for yourself against my arrival." Such was the sentiment, coolness of acting, and common conduct of all the French, from the commander-in-chief down to the humblest follower of the army.

It is surprising how the resolution and audacity of this mode of invasion paralyses the minds of men. I have heard of nations submitting quietly to a generous conqueror; but to sheath the half-drawn sword, to bend the head without a word to the yoke of violence and extortion, is an abjectness of spirit never before paralleled, I believe, in the history of man. Wherever the standard of France moved, terror and tyranny accompany it. Every street in Lisbon exhibits some sad memento of its power and oppression; for the general-in-chief, when he was here, took upon him all the authority of a conqueror, all the pride of a monarch;

On his entering public places, the company were obliged to rise and bow to him. He had his guard noble, and an almost regal establishment. He held a sort of court; a strong detachment always attended him; and two pieces of artillery with lighted matches, never left the door of his residence. The only splendour in the city was in his suite, as the inhabitants were too heart-broken and wary of awakening the rapacity of their invaders, to shew even an embroidered coat.

15

How different is the scene at present! a new existence seems to animate the city. The nobility and others are in their gayest attires: stars, fine dresses, and military uniforms of all tastes, appear in every corner of the streets. Since the total departure of the French, it is marvellous to see how many in the latter costume parade the public walks. No great proof of their true bravery, you will say, that they did not come forth so arrayed before.

But men and seasons are sadly altered with the Portuguese, since the times of their royal Juans, Alonzos, and Sebastians; and having been long out of practice in victories, no wonder when the battle comes that they should be a little shy of arms. Notwithstanding I offer an excuse for the late supineness of the once valiant Lusitorians, I cannot but be seriously surprised that it should exist. Surely the people had every stimulative to make a glorious effort: all ranks were outraged; all experienced the deepest degradation and contempt; their prince had been driven from his dominions; and the titles which their ancient noblesse had rendered sacred by deeds of valour and privations, were usurped by the *banditti* who robbed them of their liberties! yet, all was not sufficient to arouse the dormant spirit of the country.

The people murmured, but bore it. And how much longer they would have resigned themselves to dream on in this sleep of living death, I cannot guess; had not the appearance of the English and the clash of their arms awakened them to the remembrance that they were men, and had rights to preserve.

I am yet young in my knowledge of this nation; but I have my doubts whether anything like the glorious fire which now blazes throughout Spain would ever have burst forth in its sister kingdom. The Iron-rule and insinuations of the French acted like a charm upon the Portuguese; they seemed as if caught in a trap; and hopeless of release, resigned themselves to their fate, without a struggle. To prevent this possibility of resistance, their best troops were sent into France, and care taken to disarm the rest.

And sorry am I to add, that numbers of the nobility were base enough to become chains in the hands of the conqueror to enslave their country. Hence, without some foreign hand would appear to strike off their yoke, they believed it fastened on them forever. That hand has been Great Britain! The battle of Vimeira burst the rivets; Portugal is again free; and while our arm within it has power to support such an ally, I hope it will remain so. *Adieu*! Ever yours.

LETTER 2

My Dear S——

I am here still; for as yet we know nothing certain of our future movements, although reports and conjectures are in constant circulation.

A division of the army is crossing the Tagus to proceed to Elvas, but on what commission is not known. Some say the Spaniards now besieging that city refuse to acknowledge its garrison as coming under the protection of the recent convention; and that our troops are sent to direct them in their duty. If those are to be our arguments, I fear our brave allies will not consider them the gentlest in the world; and that things will alter strangely with respect to our making a friendly campaign in Spain. But this I cannot believe; the proceeding would be too absurd to deserve a moment's credit; but I report the rumour to give you an idea of the thousand fabrications which float about here in the shape of information.

I rather hail this march as a beginning of a general movement; a consummation to my hopes which is most devoutly to be wished; for longer halting here seems somewhat out of time. We are losing all the best weather; and, if we further delay, the rainy season will commence: an event which, in case of a march then; will cost us men, time, and reputation. Being under command, we must believe that our generals know best what is to be done; but, I am sorry to say, that it is a current opinion on the continent, that "a British military assistance always arrives an hour and a half too late."

In some cases this may be true; but, certainly, the remark does not stand good with regard to our arrival in Portugal. Indeed it is a question, whether or no we did not come too soon; or, at least; too scantily provided; for had we waited for a larger force, in all likelihood our united powers would have ensured repeated successes; and the result of the two glorious victories we have gained would not have been the Convention of Cintra.

As it was, after the gaining of these two battles everything was

The Field of Battle at Vimeira

expected from our arms; the Portuguese were in the highest spirits, believing that the next stroke would force Junot and his army to surrender at discretion. And, certainly, their hopes were not too sanguine, when, we recollect the able dispositions of the British troops on those memorable days; they were highly honourable to the. hero who planned them; and whose resistless execution added another bright page to the annals of Britain.

You, my good S——, know how ardently I admire, this general; and will believe the pleasure with which I read the following paragraph from the pen of Sir Harry Burrard.

> On my landing this morning (21st of August), I found that the enemy's attack had already commenced; and I was fortunate enough to reach the field of action in time to witness and approve of every disposition that had been made, and was afterwards made, by Sir Arthur Wellesley; his comprehensive mind furnishing a ready resource in every emergency, and rendering it quite unnecessary to direct any alteration.

I wish to heaven, as these sentiments must have been the sentiments of all, that all had acted corresponding to their tendency; and then our transports would not now be riding on the indignant ocean with hordes of exulting Frenchmen on board.

I have accompanied this letter with a little sketch of the ground on which the battle of Vimeira was fought. It is not drawn according to military rule; as you will be better able to form an idea of its character by a view, than by a regular plan. Let me beg of you to get the *Gazette* which contains the letter of Sir Arthur Wellesley: you will read it with double satisfaction when looking on the enclosed memorandum.

Since I began this epistle I have learnt that orders are arrived to recall Sir Hew Dalrymple; the command of the army, consequently, devolves on Sir Harry Burrard; and he, I understand, intends to remove head-quarters to Lisbon, proposing to inhabit the house lately occupied by General Junot. It belongs to a very rich diamond merchant of the name of Quintilla; whose warehouses, no doubt, added greatly to the French commander's collection of precious stones.

I believe in my former letter I mentioned that Benefecca was the residence of Sir Hew. It is a delightful, though odd looking little place; being an assemblage of handsome, mansions, and rich gardens laid out in the Dutch taste; with all the characteristics of stiff-cut myrtle trees, triangular intersections, and a most swarming population of clumsy leaden gods, nymphs, and heroes.

The convent at Benefecca is rather picturesque; and possesses one excellent picture, called a Vandyke, which it certainly is not. This valuable production had been stolen by the French collectors; and; with great perseverance, was recovered by the British officer who was entrusted with the arduous duty of answering, if possible, all the claims which the poor plundered Portuguese made for their lost property. This picture being, at length, rescued by our gallant countryman, the rejoicings, prayers, and processions of the holy brotherhood, as well as the neighbouring residents, were as great as if a descended saint had appeared amongst them; and their thanks and praises were poured forth, in so ardent a style to the officer, that I should not wonder to hear they had set him down for the next canonization.

In a magnificent valley called that of Alcantara, stands the celebrated aqueduct. In passing to Lisbon from Benefecca you behold its high expanse stretching from hill to hill. This work is of hewn stone; and is undoubtedly, a sublime monument of human ingenuity, taste, and industry: certainly, since the time of the ancients, no European production has equalled it in usefulness and grandeur. Emulative of known greatness, it forms the august union of the two heights, while its stupendous arches rise proudly across the valley; their number, I understand, is thirty-four; and they are said to be the highest in the world. The water runs in a channel along their tops; and two noble stone terraces on each side, protected by strong walls, gratify the pedestrian with the enjoyment of pure air, and a splendid and extensive view of the city, Tagus, and opposite country, On looking down into the ravine below, objects are reduced to a diminutiveness hardly conceivable. The villages, vineyards, and people, when seen from above, almost verified a description I once read of the earth's appearance when viewed from a balloon. The commencement of the last century beheld the completion of this great work.

I wish to heaven you were here to participate with me in these my rides and walks! I lose half the enjoyment by being alone; for I ever found that when, accompanied by those we regard, the relish for observation and gratification is rendered doubly sweet, put not being present, I must do as well as I can without you; and so give you, at second hand (or rather at second eyes), another prospect of Lisbon.

The best point of view whence this city and the circumjacent landscape appears to the greatest advantage is on the castle or citadel. This spot commands, in all directions, the wide Tagus covered with ships of every description, whose gay ensigns float in the languid breeze of this balmy atmosphere; and on every side you behold the romantic mountains, once the theatre of many a Moorish exploit, now clothed with Christian hamlets to their sandy feet The uneven ground on which the metropolis is built; the white aspect of its structures, broken by the black and mouldering relics of past horrors, present scenes at once interesting and picturesque. One great embellishment in all town-views is here, much wanted: the elevated tops, which in other cities are usually given to churches, palaces, and other public buildings. No large or towering edifice here strikes the eye, to break the disagreeable monotony of the undulating line of Lisbon; indeed the only objects which at all partake of the character required are the ruins of the ancient cathedral, and the beautiful convent at Buenos Ayres.

During the public rejoicings for the departure of the French I visited this last holy edifice, and also several others; but in none found any fine works of art: nothing but bad pictures appeared, great gaudiness and splendour, many lighted candles blazing in vast rows of new silver and gilt candalabrums, and the usual compliment of large chalices. Most of these articles have been lately purchased, as all their old plate being seized by the enemy was either coined into money, or is now on its way to France amongst the baggage of the departed.

In walking the streets of this capital a stranger is painfully struck with the wretchedness of its lower class: sad mementos of the effects of Gallic protection and modes of dispensing happiness! The multitude of Africans we meet at every turn is incredible, and to an English eye and smell very annoying. Their plight is not a whit better, in point of *habiliments*, than the ragged natives; and the sombre hue of their visages, with the strange discolourings they exhibit from disease and nastiness, give no very agreeable additions to the sight of a fellow creature in poverty,

However, amidst the common people, there is a race called Galicians, who are industrous, well clad, cleanly, and cheerful. Whether they come immediately from that province, or are descendants of old emigrants, I cannot pretend to say; but I am told that all of the Portuguese of whatever birthplace, who condescend to carry burthens and become thus industrous, are so denominated. The idle Lisboners proudly disdaining to bear any load but that of dirt, it. is no difficult matter to distinguish this laborious and well-dressed wholesome race from the squalid native, who would think himself insulted were you to call him a Galician. In consequence of this absurd contempt of manly toil, all the labour and profit of the day devolves on strangers: they carry the water from the fountains to the houses; are the porters of merchandise; and, in feet, monopolize all the health and decent appearance of the lower orders.

Had I come hither during the reign of the French general I could have had no opportunity of making these observations, as all traffic, commercial confidence, and security in property then took to flight, and hid themselves behind the shut-up doors and windows of their shops. But now, the spoilers gone, a renovated life seems to reanimate this lately persecuted place: the shops are again thrown open, and shine with jewellery, plate, and articles of every kind. The merchant again walks abroad, and, confident of protection, enters on new speculations; while the trading part of the city in every corner exhibits the busy faces of buyers and sellers, the proud looks of commercial consequence.

Indeed you need only cast your eyes upon the map of the world and the port of Lisbon, to see how admirably it is calculated to be a rich mart from every quarter of the globe: and as soon as the seas are open to carry to and fro the *argosies* of her merchants, her busy exchange, heaped with the products of the two Indies, and crowded with traffickers of all complexions, may remind you of the wealthy shores of Carthage, where the swarthy sons of Africa mingled with those of Europe; and, decked by the hand of commerce in all the splendours of dress, shone forth not less magnificently than their fairer brethren.

Since I am now descanting on the merits of this old capital, let me transport you back a few ages; let me introduce you to the venerable personages whom the tonsured antiquarians here say were its founders!

The city was built (so these legends tell) in the year of the world 1935 b.c.; 278 years after the deluge, by a grandson of Noah, named Elisa. What happened to it from the days of the patriarch to the Trojan war I am not prepared to relate; but while the widely wandering Ulysses was encountering his various circumstances of glory and misfortune, by good luck he landed on the chores of the Tagus, found Elisa in ruins; and being so charitable as to rebuild it while his ship's crew were probably, taking in water, new christened the restored town by the name of Ulysiponna (which derivation you may trace in its present appellation); and then sailed away with his disinterested workmen, to take a hard lodging amongst the caves of the Cyclops, It is a pity that. Homer was ignorant of this masonry of his favourite hero, as it might have afforded him a fine subject of encomium: and no doubt can be made that his poetry would have been better than the emblazoned archives of his present holy historians, to set forth the brave monarch's cunning in arts as well as in arms.

The Romans next adopted this mural offspring of two fathers: they made it a municipal city; since then, its various masters and sovereigns greatly increased its extent, and augmented its architectural beauties. Religion has done it much honour: it is the seat of a ruler in the church, called a patriarch: and became possessed of a collegiate institution, to which many of the nobility belong. So marked by the papal see was the elevation of its rank, that the patriarch was allowed to wear the dress of the pope, and the chanions that of cardinals.

Formerly, about thirty-two religious brotherhoods, and eighteen holy sisterhoods, cut off from society thousands of the useful and lovely inhabitants of this city; at present, the number of establishments of this sort are not diminished, but the professors are fewer, the recent examples in France deterring many devout persons from taking vows which a revolution might break; and those who might have chosen a cloister from motives merely prudential, regarding it as now a very uncertain asylum, turned their thoughts to other modes of maintaining a quiet existence. Indeed, the monastic rage is now so thoroughly subsided, that I have no doubt a very short time will sweep away all these detestable masses of hypocrisy and idleness, and leave men to serve God in the only proper stile, by honest industry and promoting a happy communion with their fellow creatures.

None of these consecrated structures, as public buildings, have any claim to admiration. Indeed, this pleasing state of the mind is very seldom excited by any effort of architecture crowning the banks of the Tagus. The *Place de Commercio,* in the centre of which stands an equestrian statue as bad as possible, is by far the most spacious and superb place in the town; commanding a view of the Tagus; vast ranges of *piazza* colonnade its sides, and form an agreeable walk before its shops, warehouses, private dwellings, and the room in which the mercantile exchange is held. From this magnificent spot branch the most regular and best built streets in Lisbon, many of which lead to the Rocio; the square where formerly stood a royal palace, and where now stands the Inquisition, once so terrible and iniquitous, and still a disgrace to the country.

I am sorry to say, that since the departure of the French those in power are again making its horrors the instruments of their vengeance against persons supposed to have fallen in their allegiance either to their religion or their prince.

The remains of what Lisbon was previous to the dreadful earthquake in 1755 still present themselves in many parts of the city; and certainly the complete devastation made by that tremendous catastrophe well accounts for the present barrenness of the capital with regard to public curiosities or splendid buildings. You may form an idea of the truth of my remark by the following extract from a description I the other day met with of the horrors of that ruinous scene.

> The royal palace, its fine paintings, plate, jewels, furniture, &c. &c. were all destroyed, amounting to many millions; also all the costly and ancient ornaments of the patriarchical church, as well as the riches of the palace of Braganza, wherein was kept the crown and regalia.
>
> "What escaped the convulsion of the earth was sacrificed by the flames in every part of this destined city. Most of the strong buildings fell first. The Misercordia, for the maintenance of poor female orphans, was swallowed up, together with all those unhappy virgins. The

fine church of St. Domingo, wherein one of the largest libraries in Europe was deposited, became a mass of ruins. The magnificent church of the Carmelites, with its miraculous image of our Lady of Mount Carmel, who, though present in effigy, could not save her favourite temple from destruction; together with the old cathedral establishment of the Canons of St. Augustine, supposed to be the finest piece of architecture in Christendom, and containing the ashes of King Juan the First and a long line of kings; all fell into the yawning gulf! The castle, with its archives; the prison of the Inquisition; and the Zimoira, an ancient Moorish palace, with a hundred other superb buildings of all descriptions, were lost amid the mingled horrors of fire and the earth's convulsion. Of lives, upwards of 60,000 perished.

From this sad catalogue, you will perceive that Lisbon has no attractions for the traveller, who seeks for specimens of architecture, of the fine arts, or antiquity. It is a capital of not more than fifty years standing) and, instead of being re-erected by public spirit or royal munificence, it has been huddled together by an indolent people, too indifferent to mental excellence to cultivate any genius, amongst themselves, and too jealous to allow the restoration of their city to be planned by the taste of artists from other countries. I think I must have tired you with so dismal a subject; in hopes that my next may be more amusing, I bid you a short farewell.

LETTER 3

Lisbon, October 13, 1808.

My Dear S——.

Having an opportunity of sending a letter to England, I cannot allow it to escape, although I fear my present epistle will be rather a dull one, as I am suffering under all the abominations naturally consequent on a preceding night's irregularity. Last night we gave to the nobility and others of this place as gay a ball as our taste and liberality could bestow. The opera house was the scene of our revels; and certainly, the male and female Lisbonites shone in their brightest splendour and beauty. Old and young partook of our entertainment; and, considering our clumsiness, when compared with the dexterity of other nations in managing these sort of assemblies, all went off pretty well; not forgetting to crown the whole with a superb banquet.

Foreign nations may shrug their shoulders as much as they please about the English passion for eating and drinking; but I never saw any of them (and I have seen people of all places and tongues) who do not fall too most graciously upon our teeming boards: nay, if I must speak out, 'tis my opinion that in the gormandizing talent they beat us hollow; for they not only eat with their mouths, but seem to take in the different articles of the feast with increasing appetite at nose and eyes.

I cannot help thinking that our fête was premature: certainly, the inhabitants ought to have fed the way in furnishing festivities for their: benefactors; but few nations are so fond of good fellowship as John Bull; and when he has done a good action, instead of waiting for a return, he generally follows it by a second and a third. Our friends here do not seem to wear their hearts precisely in the right place: I see no symptoms of gratitude, much less of magnificent hospitality. The characteristics of the people appear to be haughtiness, envy, and revenge; qualities which seldom fail to bring forth the monster cruelty. The lower ranks are well known for their love of taking unto themselves many things which are the property of others: a failing which is likewise father to another, the very spirit of lying.

Were we to seek a reason for these faults, I should find it in their perverted religion, moral indolence, and exclusive preference for the society of their own countrymen. The instances which writers celebrate of their bravery, generosity, and patriotism, have long been left unaugmented; but the late weight of oppression which a foreign foe laid upon the nation I hope will be the last; and, by its fellowship with England, may it learn how to value liberty, and turn the consequent circumstances to its eternal advantage! Portugal is now free! and an example of greatness is now blazing forth in the heart of Spain, which may, perchance; inspire it with the fires necessary to maintain its political existence; and awaken in the memories of her sons the recollection of the plain of Ourique, and a resolution to equal the heroism of their ancestors.

It has been a growing evil with Portugal, the assistance she has always sought m all her wars from foreign powers. Losing confidence in her own strength, she became a suspicious dependant on auxiliaries who she feared and hated, while she courted and paid them. This practice lowered the martial spirit even of the nobles; and when a military establishment was deemed necessary for the honour of the state and its defence against Spain, the government was obliged to have, recourse to officer their new regiments with foreigners from all nations, many of whom had bestowed on them the highest ranks in the Portuguese army.

Count de la Lippe was the first who at tempted to organise their military system, and to him do they owe all the little respectability it acquired; but it was a quiet fame, as the troops were never called into action. Parades and military manoeuvre were all they knew of service: year after year passed away in sleepy indolence; till, without a struggle, the whole was crushed by the overwhelming pre-eminence of France.

The departure of the prince for the Brazils (he wisely choosing a foreign realm before a home captivity), and the entire dominion usurped by the French, made the regency of Portugal a mere shadow. They had a semblance of existence, but no power. General Junot governed by military law; and he expected, nay exacted, the same respect from the nobility and people as they would pay to their lawful sovereign.

Having taken this yoke off the necks of the Portuguese, the functions of the ancient government are permitted to go on without any interference on our parts. We come to be their protectors, not their dictators; therefore, we shall soon see what is the spirit of the nation: nothing to oppress or trammel them, they have full liberty to declare their patriotism, and to come forward with whatever energy is in their hearts.

Lisbon, like almost every other continental capital, appears to an Englishman to want even common comforts. Not an inn is to be found in which you could pass the night without undergoing the tortures of a hell, almost as bad to me as flames and brimstone. I made an attempt to lodge in one; but had I been destined to pass my nocturnal hours in the most wretched hovel in England, or to have put up at this place, I should have preferred the former. It would be impossible to find in all Great Britain a habitation so ruinous, so ill furnished, so filthy, and so infested with vermin; and yet this was the Leon d'Or, the chief hotel in the city. I do not speak like one who never till now felt the difference between the warm niceness of a British inn, and the cold discomforts of a continental receptacle for travellers. I have seen much of foreign inconveniences, sufficient to render me callous to anything but the squalid nastiness of Portuguese hotels: these public mansions are not very numerous, strangers being too eager to get into lodgings, or to avail themselves of invitations from their friends, to bring these Augean stables much into use. Of course I removed my person as soon as possible, and am now quartered most pleasantly.

Mules are here used in the same proportion as in Spain, being equally fine and costly when of the first order. A hundred and fifty guineas are often given for a pair; and even a very so so animal costs twenty or thirty *monnoie d'ors*. They are far more serviceable than horses, and much less expensive to subsist: a small *cabriolé* and a couple of them, driven by a postilion, form the equipages of all, being vehicles without taste, but for use very commodious; they hold only two persons. Most people of distinction ride mules finely caparisoned, whose beauty, excepting their ungraceful length of ear, rivals the best of the native horses.

Another valuable animal here is the ox. It does all the actual labour of the country, transporting on a car of a very primitive and picturesque construction incredible loads; These creatures are yoked by the neck; the back of which, from continued rubbing against the wood that attaches the oxen to each other, becomes like the skin of a rhinoceros. The same callosity may be traced, in the mental neck, when it has long suffered itself to be borne upon by the yoke of its oppressor. The docility and ease with which these animals permit themselves to be conducted is admirable; following the peasant wherever he goes, and should he make the least angle to the right or left as he walks before them, they keep a regular march with his feet, and do not lose a step. Their bulk is not inferior to our largest oxen; and this unvaried; for amidst hundreds. I daily see, besides those which advanced with our army to Lisbon, I can perceive not one that does not accord with my description.

The car is massive and strong; of so antique a shape, that I dare say, ever since Lusitania knew the Roman jurisdiction, this machine has held its primeval form. Not only its fashion, but the temper of the people assure me of this; as they do not seem of a genius either to invent or to improve on the customs of their ancestors.

You will think that I have taken a strange prejudice against the natives; and am perhaps unfair in my estimation of their mental powers and capabilities of virtue. But look on their form of government, and that will give a reason for my disesteem of its subjects. Government is to a people what education is to a man. Salutary laws, rational liberty, and great examples, are to a nation what precepts, discipline, and good society, are to the individual. The one produces a great nation, the other a good man.

Having carried you so long on this sombre road, I must now bring you into gayer scenes, and present you to the romance-famed females of this country. I shall begin the fair procession with the lower classes: they display a surprising taste in their dress; wearing a wrapping mantle with sleeves which hang down from their shoulders. It is generally of red cloth, bound and ornamented with black velvet cut with much ingenuity. Their mode of enfolding themselves in this habit is very graceful, and attracts much attention, as the whole form of the figure is seen, finished by a neat foot and ankle. These extremities of their persons are very pretty, and adorned with the nicest care: when the filth of the streets is considered, one is amazed at the universal cleanliness with which this national mark of female pride is preserved. Their heads are enveloped in a white handkerchief, out. of which peeps an interesting, though sallow countenance, with a pair of fine dark eyes. Such is the *tout ensemble* of a Lisbon beauty.

The higher orders, by a strange contradiction, though perhaps possessing an equally fine foot and ankle with their humbler sisters, pay very little attention to this part of their persons; and, in fact, the fashion of their dress throughout is inferior to the elegant simplicity of the fair plebeian. I say elegant in form; I do not mean always in state or materials, as they are often, as you will remember I have before hinted, both ragged, coarse, and dirty; all abandoned to the national infirmity, but the pretty foot and leg.

There is a middle class which array themselves in black lace veils and cloaks. These females have a neat appearance; and are generally followed by an old woman, a sort of *duenna*, who keeps a respectful distance from her fair charge.

The nobility seldom go out in the day; and when they do, it is in their carriages to pay visits, or to hear mass. Hence, entertainments, or church, are the only opportunities a stranger has of seeing the females of the equestrian orders. However, since the French brought their own manners into this capital, less ceremony has been used; and the ancient custom of the ladies being so constantly kept *a la Turc,* is declining rapidly: a great blessing to the fair prisoners, as well as a gratification to the traveller; who can say he has seen half a nation only, when the most beautiful part of it is immured from his eyes,

I cannot speak in commendation of their powers for conversation. The best parts of female education are here not much attended to; therefore our evening amusements, when we are so honoured as to be admitted of their parties, are generally cards and dancing, but nothing else; for though they always conclude the evening with a supper, it is a repast of which, with them, they have never allowed us to partake. Their hour of dinner is about three o'clock; though some have fallen so far into the English fashion as to make it five.

As to the sincerity of their devotion, I fear it is not very great. The observations I made while at church seemed to tell me that the fair worshippers came to pay a very different homage from that of the temple. Indeed, I cannot wonder that they should forget to whom the sacred building is dedicated, when they turn about and look at its furniture—Imagine a mob of strangely attired figures to represent saints; and Virgin Marys, dressed in Gothic habits, stiff sacks, and fine brocaded petticoats, gazing at you with bedaubed faces, and lighted up on all sides with long and glimmering candles. These, with a hundred objects, present themselves, which call forth any ideas but those of religious awe and respect.

Processions and ceremonies are passing to and fro without end. No day escapes but what you witness whole trains of monks, accompanied by swarms of idle people, traversing the streets in every direction. Independent of these personages, groups of singers bearing baskets, and begging in couples, interrupt your walks.

Yesterday eight or ten large cars, containing empty copper boilers, and drawn by fat oxen decorated with branches of olive trees, trailed in funeral order about the city. They were preceded by about sixty ill and well-dressed persons, a few monks, and many other people bearing conveniences for collecting loaves from the charitable, in order to make soup for the unprovided. The collection made, the cooking afterwards publicly took. place on a spot near one of the holy edifices; around which attended hundreds of naked, ragged, lame, lazy, and disgusting wretches, each armed with their various means of receiving the steaming concoction.

Amidst the other unpleasant objects that daily occur, and which you might stumble over, is an accumulation of a different kind from the piles of filth I before noticed as occupying the streets, and much more offensive; namely, the bodies of dead dogs, cats, and horses. The hot weather and rain reduce them to the most horrid state; and set all sorts of infernal smells afloat to annoy our senses. In taking a rather circumscribed ride, I observed no less than five dead horses; some that had recently expired, and others which had been long enough deceased to be half worried by the flies, birds, and prowling canine race.

Thus you see, from the obstinate perversions of their religion, and the bad state of the police, that idleness is encouraged, filth fostered, and a thousand pestilential disorders engendered. The climate of Lisbon is by no means unfriendly to the birth of all the horrid train of pain and woe. At present it is extremely hot: the evenings are chilly; and a heavy dew is perceptibly seen and felt, rendering the person who is so imprudent as to venture into the air subject to sudden and serious indispositions. From these considerations, I cannot but be surprised that Lisbon is recommended as a proper place for invalids of the most delicate kind. Think but of the atmosphere impregnated with horrors of every sort; recollect the total want of every comfort necessary for the sick; and then say, why is the unhappy creature fading under the cruel grasp of a consumption sent hither? Were physicians to prescribe the neighbourhood of Lisbon, instead of Lisbon itself, to their patients, they might do some good: for, at some distance from this disease-clouded city, the air is pure and serene.

So much for civil, now for martial news. Our army is marching in three columns towards Spain. Twenty-one thousand men compose this force. Sir John Moore is their commander-in-chief; Sir Harry Burrard remaining here. A few troops with brigadier-general Stewart go to Oporto; and the regiments of the German Legion, with some others, amounting to about seven or eight thousand men, remain to garrison the town and forts of Lisbon. Happy am I, now that a prospect presents itself of our fighting another Vimeira. I hope a victory will be the subject of the next letter from your friend.

P. S. As you will be curious to know how we advance, I enclose you the state of our columns.

LETTER 4

Lisbon, October 19th, 1808.

My dear S———.

I intend remaining in this city some few clays longer; purposing to overtake the troops before they advance far into Spain. By this little delay I shall certainly find more comforts in the towns I may pass through, than if with the army. You will naturally imagine that the pleasures of society, or the fascinations of a softly-struck guitar, have detained me. But no; a particular friend of mine is suddenly too unwell to travel. When he recovers, which I hope will be soon, we shall commence our march together. During the interval, I intend visiting Cintra, Mafra, &c.

With respect to amusements; balls, parties, and other things of a similar sort, occupy our evenings. I wish I could say that the drama was amongst them. That art is like many others here which require mental exertions, at a very low ebb. They have two theatres, it is true; but then the question is, what are they? The opera once was very well sustained; indeed, in no way inferior to our own, or to the most celebrated on the Continent. A few months ago several excellent dancers were brought hither, and ballets were produced in great splendour. But this was under the regime of the late French governors of Lisbon; with them, departed some of the best performers; and so this species of amusement has ceased.

I am told that an application had been made, to the British commandant here to sanction the re-establishing the *corps d'opera*: but he, with the true spirit of the cause he had engaged in, refused having anything to do with it. Our object in occupying Portugal, was far different from the French; we did not wish to distract their attention by vain shews; but, if possible, to concentrate all their thoughts on the grand object of maintaining the freedom we had given them. Hence, to ask us to fill their city with diversions, was to empty their camps; and fasten on again the chains we had unloosened. A country struggling for liberty should reject with a jealous disdain all that would withdraw its thoughts from the great and general cause.

I went the other evening with a very pleasant family to the Salitro theatre. Its entertainment consists of three pieces. One of them was a ballet. Most of the performers were Portuguese; and seemed to place the perfection of their elastic art in the force and height from which they sprung from the ground, cutting, certainly, an unparalleled number of capers in the air.

The female dancers were all well formed, with perfectly beautiful legs and feet. Every motion was wonderfully light and dexterous, and yet totally devoid of grace or delicacy. The latter want is very apparent by the constant state of the lower extremities, which these *volant* ladies never allow to be one moment covered. No very moral, no more than modest display; for the partial glimpse at so perfect an object, while the nymph so exerts herself, seldom fail to create in the warm fancies of most men the most riotous ideas; while the colder temperated mortals regard her with the utmost disgust and contempt.

Whether the nobler class seriously approve of this exposure I cannot say; but I observed, that whenever a leg, or somewhat higher, was made particularly apparent, it was hailed by the most vociferous acclamations. I think, one small proof that the *noblesse*, and those approximating to the equestrian order, do not dislike the wanton taste, is the universal adoption of a dance which originated in South America. It has even descended to the lowest classes, as all the peasants foot it to their guitars. It resembles the primitive dances of most savage nations; being a performance between a man and a woman, who sing, and twist their persons in every possible indecent position; advancing to each other, and retreating occasionally, with all the indelicacy of action and grimace conceivable; figurative of rites which disgrace any art employed to commemorate them either for private or public gratification.

During my observance of an amiable pair thus employed, whilst exerting their agile persons to the best of their lascivious conceptions, I begged to know the sentiments of their song. I put my question to a lovely woman who sat next me (O *pudor*! that a fair and modest female should be brought to such a sight!): she replied, "I am happy for the character of the nation that you do not understand our language. The words speak but the depravity of another art: you can easily judge by their action what is the meaning of their song."

This then is the *acmé* of Portuguese theatrical taste; and if of their taste, of their morals—fogh! the subject is too disgusting to dwell on.

There is another theatre, not far from the square in which stands the Inquisition, where merely comedies are performed, and pieces of great import. I passed a stupid evening there, indeed a very disagreeable one; for not a few of our naval heroes, who had drank too freely of the juice of the grape, placed themselves on each side of the stage, and were no very quiet neighbours to the poor actors. I am happy to see an order from our military governor to prevent such exhibitions in future; as interruptions of the performance, and *fracas*, were usually the consequence.

If the weather prove fine, I purpose going almost immediately to Cintra, the Switzerland of Portugal; after which I shall prepare for my departure for the army. General Moore has not yet left us, but we daily expect his march also.

While thus determining, I cannot but, put up my prayers that the wet season may be averted for some time, and not overtake us on our route. The consequences to the army would be dreadful. Rain here is not like rain with you. Compared with us, the heaviest showers descend on your head like dews: but here (and I have felt two or three specimens) the rain pours down in floods, like torrents from a waterfall. Tremendous as these deluges are, they are the safety of the city; for in an hour, they wash away all the filth into the capacious bosom of the Tagus.—*Adieu*!

LETTER 5

Lisbon, October 29th, 1808.

Dear S——,

I promised you an account of my trip to Cintra; though circumstances checked my observations, and consequently lessened my means of giving you pleasure, I shall keep my word.

I commenced my journey with the most heavenly weather;

but, before I had reached the Lusitanian *arcadia*, a melancholy change took place in the atmosphere, and I arrived under a heavy storm of rain. As my time was limited, and the present obstacle to a fine view no inconsiderable one, I was obliged to make the best of my calamity, and not allow it to prevent me gleaning at least a few of the minor beauties of this lovely spot.

It is rightly named the Switzerland of this part of the continent; and its valleys and richly clothed heights form a luxuriant contrast to the burnt, arid and barren tracks in its neighbourhood; Many romantic dwellings, belonging to nobility and merchants, are scattered about, and greatly animate the scene. Indeed, to a lover of nature nothing can be mere enviable than a residence amid these beauteous hills and valleys. It seems the very garden of the sylvan deities; and I have no doubt, would be found the fountain of health also, were invalids to seek its pure and ambrosial air rather than the fetid and pestilential atmosphere of Lisbon.

Besides, the inn, when compared with others, is excellent; to advantage very essential to the comfort of travellers, and indispensable when they are sick. Good as it is now, they tell me it was better formerly, when its first foundress still held the keys: she was an Irish woman; but having realized a large fortune; has retired from the bar to the more extensive field of the vintage. Another person has taken the inn, and she has commenced trafficker in a species of wine made near here, which is much celebrated, and is not at all inferior to Burgundy.

Picture to yourself, in miniature, the most interesting parts of the country this *endroit* resembles, and you will have a complete portrait of Cintra. Its living objects differ sadly from the landscape. No beauty, no taste, no animation appear in their looks, garbs, and actions: they walk about as if totally insensible of the paradise in which they dwell. I mean the lower class of natives; of the higher, as I did not visit any of their villas, I had no opportunity of judging.

The weather continued so adverse, that, giving up any farther views as hopeless, I returned speedily to Lisbon, not having seen one half of what I wished. Amongst my heaviest disappointments I include that of not being able to reach Mafra; so celebrated for its extensive palace, library, and convent, There was a holy edifice at Cintra, called the Cork Convent, which the storm prevented me from visiting, hence my mortification was doubled. Every article of furniture, &c. in this building is formed of cork, and must have a very curious effect. It stands upon a height, and in fine weather commands an admirable prospect.

Yesterday Sir John Moore and suite left this capital. We shall follow in a day or two, and hope to overtake the army before it reaches Salamanca, or Valladolid at farthest. In equipping myself for the march, it was necessary to purchase both mules and horses. Of the latter I had only one; but now, were you here I could introduce you to a very handsome stud. During my traffic for them, I discovered in all the sellers that insatiable passion for extortion which, I am sorry to find (from meeting it everywhere), is an absolute vice of human nature. The Portuguese merchants seemed to think that they could not better express their gratitude for the services we had rendered them, than by lightening our purses at every opportunity. Honesty was never the measurer of their price; for they generally exacted five times the real value of the article in question.

This evil has been augmented by the readiness with which we comply with their demands; and that it is so we daily experience, in the increasing prices of every necessary we wish to buy. Indeed, I have always observed that wherever the English have been repeated travellers, entertainment at inns, &c. is doubly expensive. Landlords, tradesmen, and even men of nobler callings, make our thoughtless countrymen their prey; some from an inordinate avarice, that cares not by what means it gathers wealth, and others from an idea which all foreigners entertain, that an English toiler is inexhaustible. And this latter sentiment is not likely to lose ground, while so many of our brethren foolishly and blindly throw away their gold, without scruple or investigation.

Having had a little experience during my campaigns in life abroad, I did not now allow myself this British licence: and when I found that all my endeavours to purchase at a reasonable price were abortive, I left the business to my servant, whose honesty, as well as acuteness, is, perhaps, unequalled; I am sure it cannot be excelled. He speaking the language well, and not being an Englishman, succeeded admirably; and in a few hours

I had in my stable a pair of excellent mules, with all their appointments, for twenty *monnoie d'ors*; about one hundred and twenty dollars. For these same animals, had I gone to make the bargain myself, most probably I should have been obliged to have given exactly three or four times the sum.

Aware of the liberality of the English, temptations for expenditure wooed us from every side of Lisbon. The *Place de Commercio* was (or rather is) an absolute vanity fair, silver and gold worked into the most fantastic shapes, and interwoven with the precious gems of the Brazils, attract your eyes as *nouvelle* ornaments, crosses, chains, rings and bracelets. We purchase them in loads, to send home to our fair friends; and the Portuguese, complimenting us on our taste, &c. say, "They never before saw their shops so full of jewellery, none, indeed, was ventured into sight during the presence of the French: so powerful is the talisman of safety and honour."—A talisman to be sure we find our virtues; but not like Aladdin, to conjure up valuable commodities unpaid for.

The contemplation of this nation is highly flattering to our dignities: our presence alone seems bulwark sufficient for them; and notwithstanding the short time we have been on their shores; they calculate on their independence being secure; they already talk of the return of their prince, as of an event that is certain. I hope in heaven these fond hopes may be realized; but as the shoulder must. be laid to the wheel, as well as Jove bid it move, unless the Portuguese determine to defend themselves, they will as little deserve to escape the chains of France, as they would be likely to effect it.

All seems ceremony with this people: they talk of bravery, and none prove themselves greater cowards: they profess religion, and none are greater formalists. Witness in both instances, the readiness with which they yielded to the French usurpation-the avidity with which they banquet on all the impurities of their satyr-like amusements. As far as encomiums on British valour, and their own fine uniforms will go, they are brave soldiers; as far as church ceremonies will carry them, they are good Christians. *Te deum*s and holy processions are the present business of their lives.

At one of their principal places of devotion three or four sermons were preached, and several grand pieces of music performed, to invoke the canonized calendar in our behalf. Every star, riband, and brocade coat and petticoat attended; and, as it was expected that our commanders, and officers of rank, naval and military, would be present, accordingly, the first day they acceded to the general wish; but finding the orations possessed more of earth than fire, and that the music seemed mere in unison with the lengthened notes of the spheres, than with their harmony, this first visit was the last of our commanders. They made their bow to the St. Cecilia and the St, Mary of the church together, to the no little disappointment of the *noblesse*, who gave the festival rather as a festivity to their protectors than as a religious feast. A strange practice this, you will think, of weighing a pious duty against an English ball!

In the course of my frequenting these churches, I could not but observe, that during divine service the female part of the congregation, as I before hinted, are rather heathen in their worship; paying more oblations to the god of love than to all the saints of the calendar, the frozen-hearted Anthony inclusive. And it is perfectly true, that tender *rendezvous* and casual acquaintances are here continually made, to the same amorous purpose.

Indeed, I know many of my brother officers have paid daily attendance to these gentle priestesses of the smiling deity, and have come away without complaining of their frowns. We may trifle with these subjects, my friend, when we treat of them on a foreign shore; but did we see such sacrilegious use of our churches—did we see the hearts of our virgins polluted, even in the temples of holiness, how would we execrate the idle pomps which, by addressing the senses alone, left the soul unoccupied, a prey to every idle intruder! But, with my spurs on my feet ready for the march, I have not time to moralize: a moment or two to finish this gadding letter, and then I shall be gone. The church of St. Roque is richly ornamented; and often fully and prettily attended. It is celebrated for a chapel dedicated to St. John, wholly composed of Mosaic work. The pictures in this art are exquisite; the brilliancy of their colours being not inferior to that of oil. Specimens of rare marbles, and fine gilt bronze, as well as masses of wrought silver, decorate this hallowed little place. The most valuable of these treasures were buried during the sojourn of their French protectors; but, as soon, as we arrived, they, as well as a range of huge candelabras, were brought again to the light of day.

I have been desirous to visit the interior both of the convents and monasteries; but I have not had time to persevere in seeking an opportunity, and chance has not been kind enough ever to conduct me on any of their holy fêtes to the church door. The male members of these institutions prowl about the streets continually; their long robes, large hats, and dirty beards, forming a strange contrast to our gay uniforms and highland garbs. I must confess I feel a Briton's pride when I look from these miserable sons of squalid uselessness to the active graces of our English soldier, to the sturdy health of our dauntless Scot. May such ever be the feelings of a Briton! at home, they are my satisfaction; abroad, my boast; and in the field, my glory.

Tomorrow we set forth to follow the army. To have all in order, I had my cavalry and force paraded; and I assure you, from their number and respectability, I begin to imagine myself a leader of no little consequence. My friend, too, is not less ably appointed; and when we unite our suites, *en route,* a very formidable caravan will present itself. As soon as we halt, you shall hear again from yours.

LETTER 6

Abrantes, Nov.7th, 1808.

My Dear S——.

We left the extraordinary city of Lisbon on the 3rd instant. Well may I give it that epithet; for it was the only, city in which I had ever sojourned that I quitted without regret.

It was our intention to proceed by easy marches. We were admirably mounted, and, our servants provided with every convenience in the same way. Our horses and mules numbered ten, in all, besides our followers, who had four.

From our military mode of travelling, it is out of my power to make you acquainted with the obstacles and other discomforts which may arise to private individuals making a tour through this country or Spain. We had nothing to do with public accommodations; but on entering town or village received from the magistrates billets on the best and richest inhabitants. In compliance with this authority, they were obliged not only to admit us, but to furnish us with lodgings for our whole suite.

And to do them justice, we have been treated with the courtesy of visitants: their politeness and hospitality never allowed us to remember that our quarters had been yielded to a command.

This premised, I shall now conduct you with us through the places we visited on our way to this town. You must not expect much gay amusement in a soldier's annals, but if it affords you any, I shall be repaid for my disinterestedness in thus devoting time to you which I steal from sleep.

I shall begin with our leaving Lisbon; and, as is generally the case with me, it was a few hours after the time fixed for our departure, before we got well underway. In faith, I must confess that unless military necessity obliges, I know no set of men more indolent in putting themselves in motion than those belonging to the army. It was three o'clock in the afternoon of the 3rd *ultimo* ere we were fairly launched: if I may make use of such a metaphor, for a troop of merry cavaliers taking their course towards the laurel-springing plains of Spain.

It being so late, we proposed halting at Sacavam, a place distant about two leagues. The road is paved with large stones, which does not promote the ease of travelling; in carriages, it must be intolerable. However, while your body is tormented, your mind would be amused by the surrounding landscape. The country is pretty, and finely enriched with gardens belonging to the villas in the vicinity of the metropolis,

Reaching Sacavam, nothing either for beauty or interest claimed our particular attention, and we left it early next morning to pursue our way.

We passed a branch of the Tagus on a sort of flying bridge; and after winding round a toll, we opened into an extensive plain, which extended itself to the very edge of the narrowing river. A range of high and luxuriantly clothed mountains rose from this flat. Their hold and romantic forms, abounding in the dark olive tree, finely contrasted by the pale green pine, gave a striking sublimity to the scene. The sombre hue of the hills, their impenetrable shades, and wildly fantastic shapes, seemed the very seat of Cervantes' genius; and every moment I expected to see the mad Cardenio rush from the thickets, and standing on the steep, discourse most eloquently of love and tyrant man.

The whole line of the country on the right of the road (as we proceeded) is intersected with salt manufactories. The material is produced from the marshes, which are drained, and the saline particles carefully collected and formed into pyramidical piles. They appear at a little distance like a small encampment. The country continues flat, on the left of us, till we approach Elvas; producing abundance of corn, as well as pasture for cattle. Vast stacks of corn rose in innumerable places like small cities.

Villa Franca closed this day's march, a distance of five leagues. It is a small but pretty town, celebrated for its vineyards and press for the port wine. The season was advanced beyond our wishes; the juice of the grape had already been extracted; and we were deprived of seeing a process which would have been particularly gratifying to a people who drink so largely of their labours. Early in October is the time of vintage; and during that period the scene in and about the town is extremely busy, and well worthy the visitation of a stranger.

In this place we experienced hospitality in the warmest degree; and the next morning resumed our route towards Cartaxo; a march of six leagues. Here again we passed over a regularly paved highway. The roads are so made to prevent their being swept away in the rainy season. The hedges (if so I may be allowed to stile them) were composed of the different species of aloe. Many were at that time in full bloom. The stem shoots up to about twelve or fourteen feet from the centre of the form we see them in, when young in England. At the extremity of this, the flowers ramify on every side, wearing in shape, at some distance, the appearance of a Scotch fir-tree. I observed that most of those which had produced this centurial flower were dying; so that a hundred years decides the existence of this venerable plant.

Here the road became very sandy (a soil in which the aloe thrives best), and wound its course over the hills, through an extensive forest of cork, pine, and olive trees; leaving, as we ascended, the dark waters of the Tagus, and the vast plain beneath stretching to a distance beyond our ken.

The quarters prepared for us at Cartaxo had been occupied by a French general when his army was advancing towards Lisbon. Our host, whose hatred of France only seemed to be equalled by his gratitude to England, amused us with recitals of the abominable insolence of his last military guest. One half of his narrative was so disgraceful *a la grande nation* and to man, that I neither could nor would believe it. However, there were a few complaints not quite so improbable, as the like conduct had been exhibited before; namely, that these Gallic heroes obliged the lord of the mansion to become their valet, to assist in pulling off their boots, and to perform every other duty of that branch of servitude. Not satisfied with using the master of the house as their slave, they appropriated the property as their own, taking away with them the silver spoons, and whatever else tempted their avidity,

This town has not much to boast, either in situation or buildings. The only one of any magnitude is a convent at the entrance, fitted with idle and dirty monks, who possess the same excuse for want of hospitality with half the continent—that the French had robbed them of all their treasures. This plea is often resorted to by the laity as well as the priesthood; an argument very disadvantageous to our poor troops when they are so unfortunate as to be quartered on any of these niggardly gentry. Cartaxo is celebrated for making a wine of a peculiar excellence: I have drank it in England under the appellation of white claret. The common *vin du paye* is very good; and I have little doubt, but with very small additions of port and brandy, we consume many hundred pipes of it in London under the name of genuine port.

The approach of winter is very apparent. The more tender trees are losing their leaves, and the whole face of the *verdured* country becoming dark and brown; a hue which it does not lose until the rainy season has pretty copiously discharged its floods. This melancholy and dreaded time has been expected for some weeks; an event which must prove very detrimental to our march, both as to the expedition and health of the troops; for, I understand, the torrents rush from the mountains upon the valleys and plains with such: violence as to render the roads scarcely passable; swelling the rivers beyond their bounds, bearing away the bridges, and creating a dangerous damp throughout the whole of the surrounding atmosphere.

Had we commenced our march some weeks ago, these evils would not have threatened us: the elements in our favour, we should have had. nothing to contend against but the foe; but now, I fear, that the approaching season will destroy more men than the bullet

The city of Santoram was the next place in which we took up our quarters; it being distant from Cartaxo only two leagues. The country is extremely hilly; and the appearance of the city from the last height we mounted before we reached it is beautifully picturesque. It is built on a high and commanding situation, proudly overlooking the far-stretching plains beneath, through the bosom of which rolls the Tagus; whose yellow edges, shaded by dark groves of olive trees, gild the long expanse, enlivened with spreading vineyards and large fields of Indian corn. These objects enrich with fine variety the aspect of this part of the country, while the blue heads of lofty mountains in the distance raise a majestic boundary to the landscape.

The town possesses large religious edifices, with a handsome square, and is encircled by extended fortifications. Its natural situation is extremely strong: the side on the south-east is dangerously steep; and I make no doubt has been the theatre of many a hard-fought contention between the Moors and Portuguese. Specimens of the architecture of the former people present themselves in all quarters; a splendid monument of their power; and a warning to the present inhabitants how they permit the settling of evaders, who will soon reign as tyrants over the people which suffer themselves to be enslaved.

We passed through this, city; and when we descended into the plain, the rain set in so thick and heavy as to form a veil between us and the surrounding objects. Hence we lost many a noble feature of the country; and after a tedious and wearisome march of seven hours, found ourselves at Golega: found, I say justly say, for it was like feeling our way in the dark; so blinding was the watery tempest that blew around. At this place we came up with the rear of the army. Though the circumstance might increase the animation of our future scenery, it certainly did not add to our prospect of accommodation. The greater the number of claimants, the less likely were we to be well-appointed in lodgings and board.

But these considerations, though of consequence with the mere traveller, to the soldier are of secondary moment. If we have a shelter from the weather, with a little wholesome food, and a clean truss of straw to sleep on, these are comforts sufficient for the sons of Mars. But should a decent bed and a spread table await us, then that is luxury. These are sentiments

VALE OF TANCOS

with which all soldiers, of whatever rank, ought as necessarily provide themselves, &c. with swords or firelocks. But we have not, as yet, had much call for this military philosophy.

Golega, though very crowded, greeted us with the same hospitality we had met at our last halting-place, and allowed us to want for nothing. The weather prevented us from passing beyond the door. Pleasure may be postponed, but duty must be obeyed: so, early next day, under a desperate rain, we renewed our journey. Not far from Golega we crossed a small but rapid river on a bridge of pontoons; on the opposite bank rose the town of Punheté and, for as much as we could discern through the weeping atmosphere, it seemed prettily built.

Continuing our course by the river, and occasionally losing its windings by mounting the succeeding hills over which the road lay; during a favourable moment, while on one of these commanding heights, a short cessation happened of the showers, and discovered a most enchanting view. The Tagus rolling through a bold and rocky range of hills; the dark cork and olive shrouding their antiquated bosoms; even hanging their impending tops to the very brink of the river, excepting where abrupt projections of the stony precipices pushed forward in sterile majesty.

The village of Tancos stands at the foot of the mountain we were descending. Its rustic buildings, and one or two religious edifices, rose from amidst the trees; which, with; the busy advance of the troops, and the laden wagons appearing and losing themselves in the deep windings of the road, formed a scene which combined all the grandeur of nature with objects similar to those which so often glittered on these heights in the chivalric ages of Christian and pagan warfare.

On the opposite shore the view was still more romantic; rude and savage in its character; its dark and gloomy immenses overshadowed a lofty rock which stood proudly and alone in the midst of the rapid stream. Its summit is crowned with the remains of an ancient Moorish fortress; the mouldering walls and battlements of which still more impress the beholder's fancy with the wild and heroic times of *Durendarte and Balermo!* The heavens shone in unison with the whole; and the shade of the heavy and impending clouds spread a tone over the view, inspiring a nameless horror.

Leaving this apt region for romance, we journeyed on to Abrantes; at which city we arrived very late, and yet too soon for the civilities of our reception: here we halt a day, hoping the wet weather will abate; and not only promise us drier jackets in our next march, but enable us, while we remain, to traverse the beauties of the town. Beauties! so you see my imagination always runs a gay path before it comes to sober reality. I put forth my scrutinizing gaze into the streets and habitations, and met. nothing in return but filth, deformity, and grumbling.

The place is large, ruinous and miserable; full of poverty, and, what is worse, discontent. The present duke has not been idle in sowing-seeds of disloyalty to their country amongst these ignorant people. Indeed, it is a very easy matter to corrupt the judgements of the wretched; none will be faithful in spite of wants and temptations but the well-principled. Hence we cannot be surprised that the suffering and uneducated of every country should be ready to receive the gold, and adopt the arguments of France. Sovereigns must begin at the right end of policy; and open the eyes of their lowest subjects to the true estimates of vice and virtue, actual necessities, and fantastic wants, before they can expect their people to be steadfast in their duty through all the sophistries of the present times.

Such a mode of keeping men in order is the cheapest and the surest; it is better than military law, for the guard is within themselves. Were the Irish peasants properly educated, popery would gradually disappear; and the crown have a whole nation of brave and faithful subjects, instead of the miserable and discontented bands who now fill England with suspicion and devices for punishment. Teach Ireland that it is her interest to be loyal, and she will soon make it her duty. Mr. Lancaster's plan of education is a cheap, a comprehensive, and efficient one to accomplish these purposes. But to return to Abrantes.

Its situation is fine; being on a high hill; and might have excited our admiration, had not the pelting of the pitiless storm rendered our ascent fatiguing and miserable to the last degree. Within the walls, the reception we met with was a continuation of the same cold and damping welcome we had received from its ever-teeming clouds. In short, Abrantes is the first place in Portugal (and for the honour of the country I hope it will be the last) where we have found any difficulty in obtaining quarters.

The number of our troops was the excuse; and we might have given some credence to the plea, had we not been so hospitably and cheerfully billeted in the preceding towns. The tardiness of the magistrate augmented our disgust; for he left us two full hours on horseback, standing under torrents of rain, before he chose to find us even hovels to shelter. My party, being wet through, were, at last, shown into a naked and wretched house, without the appearance of fire, or any other comfort. Exhausted as we were, with great difficulty we compelled an old Hecate-like dame to produce us beds; and if we had not threatened to put our domestics to bed to her, they must have shared those of our horses and mules.

The next day. was but a repetition of the preceding, as an incessant deluge frustrated my perambulating intentions. From this city one of the noblest families in Portugal takes a title, which is now bestowed by Napoleon on General Junot. Here are the remains of an extensive castle: also many convents well filled, and still in maturity; and a public square of some consequence. Not long since the great national entertainment, a bullfight, was given here; I wish it had been my good fortune to have been present. The constituents of these amusements, though remnants of barbarous courage, are yet mementos of the spirit which cleared the forest of its savage inhabitants; and drove the feet of invasion far from their shores. There is as much difference in the principles which lead to the bullfight, and to the bull-baiting, as between the contest of two wrestlers, and the brutal blows with which the tyrant beats his slave to the ground. Tomorrow we renew our march; and not sorry shall I be to shake the dust off my feet which belongs to the inhospitable city of Abrantes.—Ever yours.

LETTER 7

Zibrira, November, 1808.

The sun smiled upon us, and not through tears, the morning we left Abrantes. As we descended the hills, an extensive and magnificent view spread before us. But our route soon became more enclosed; and we found ourselves amongst the ravines of innumerable mountains, whose hollows abounded with luxuriant olive trees and the wild arbutus. The beautiful arms of that sweet plant gave brightness to the scene, while its flowers and fruit yielded a most delightful refreshment both to the eye and palate.

The farther we penetrated these tremendous piles of earth, their aspects became more stony and desolate; and had we not been travelling in such intimidating characters, the desert silence of the scene, its terrific recesses, and solitary wastes, might have made us tremble for our safety.

One track we mounted, bold and hazardous as the precipices, of St. Gothard, and not at all inferior in sublimity. The rolling streams which dashed from every chasm or time-worn furrow in the rock, were rendered doubly romantic by the thick chestnut-trees that overhang their edges; the autumnal tints of their yellow leaves made a fine contrast with their sober-hued neighbours, the cork and the olive.

The cork-tree so nearly resembles the oak in form and branching, even to a similar acorn, that, for some time, I mistook it for the same. When age has given the bark sufficient thickness for use, the natives peel it off from the bottom of the trunk up as high as the lowest limbs will permit; and when time recovers the naked wood with a clothing not inferior to the first, it is again stripped, and left to acquire new *habiliments*. So useful is this natural production, that even furniture is made of it; and in most of the cottages, you see chairs and tables of no other composition; to a stranger they appear heavy in the extreme, but on raising them from the ground, the sensation is extraordinary on discovering their wonderful lightness. Roofs of dwellings are, in many places, laid over with this vegetable substance; it being found an impenetrable preservative against the sweeping torrents which deluge this country in the rainy months.

I cannot give you any interesting account of the costume of this part of the world; the peasantry have no peculiar habit; the most characteristic mark is, that one colour of a dark brown is the universal hue of their apparel; the material is generally cloth; and of this is made jacket, breeches, and gaiters. These, with a large hat and cloak over their shoulder, complete their dress. The females exhibit nothing to attract particular notice but their extreme neglect of all cleanliness, and total want of all beauty; not even a tawdry attempt at taste ever appears to vary the sad surface; all is one sombre mass of dirt; a very sympathizing covering with such rugged efforts of nature.

Villa del Rea was the halting-place we had fixed on for that day's rest. It is a small village in the heart of the mountains, standing naked and treeless, We found the captain-major, or chief person in the place, very civil. He lodged us, fed us, and performed every act of humble hospitality with the most active zeal. During our evening meal we were visited by the staff of this colony, *viz*. the apothecary and the priest, besides a train of villagers who filled our room, staring and smoking, and sending forth an odour which stopped the action of our mouths that we might defend our noses.

Our patience of these rustic intruders, certainly gained in comparison with that of our Gallic predecessor who, so far from allowing them to pollute the respirations of their imperial lungs, chased the natives away from within a hundred yards of their dwellings and if any dared to draw near, answered his curiosity with the flat of a sword or a stick.

The next day we left our host impressed with a high idea of our merits, and full of prayers for our success. Seeing our retinue off, we resumed the march, and made our slow advances to the nearest village, called Cortazados, four leagues distant. By the way, I must apprise you that these same leagues are the longest divisions of that name I ever travelled; four good English miles and a half would but scantily make up a Portuguese *league*. I am told that in Spain they are shorter; I hope it may prove so, else we have a most tremendous march in perspective before we come up with the main body of the army, should they be destined to halt at Valladolid ere they advance to Burgos.

The road led along the tops of the hills; and with here and there an exception, was tolerably good; as both artillery and cavalry might keep on without difficulty. Droves of goats hung on the brows of the adjacent eminences; while, at their feet, an oxen-drawn plough was seen dragging its industrious share through the scanty soil. The rustic pursuit below, and the rugged scene above, uniting in one picture the contrary charms of cultivation and of wild nature.

At Cortazados we were wretchedly accommodated; but, at least, not worse than the inhabitants, for there was scarcely a dwelling in the place that deserved the name of a house. The people expressed willingness to oblige, and lamented much that the

French pillagers in their advance to Lisbon had robbed them of almost every means to serve us. Owing to this, it was with difficulty we procured corn for our cattle; and even for the little we did collect we paid exorbitantly.

During our march we were frequently shewn the caps and arms of the unfortunate Frenchmen who had fallen sacrifices to the knives of this oppressed people, They told us exultingly, while they held them up, the particulars of many a bloody scene; and how often it had been repeated by the discovery and murder of some other poor stragglers. I fear that this base sort of revenge is the only one the generality of this nation are now capable of devising.

I nowhere hear amongst them any sentiments on their release from a foreign yoke, which speak principles of a nobler kind than a merely natural joy at being relieved from insult and ex-action. No grand views connected with freedom and national advantages seem to enter their heads; all they think of is the temporary escape from personal inconvenience; and I have a notion that had Napoleon's generals acted with less rigour, and condescended in any degree to have won the people's confi-dence, we should have heard that all was very quietly settled in Lusitania. But when the titled of the native nobility are as-sumed, and their estates sequestrated. When the lower classes are oppressed and plundered; no wonder then that everybody being injured, all should seek redress; and, fearful of their own strength, fly to the broad shield of England.

Five leagues from our present sojourn were to bring us to Saza-dos. We set forth, and the weather proving good, enjoyed many noble scenes; the prospect was like the former, mountainous, with every varied form of alpine and yet bolder character. The general aspect of the view readied to me, though with a gi-gantic resemblance, the sublimest parts of North Wales. And if this colossal country possessed a few lakes, it would have in all things the advantage; as the richness of its valleys are beauties which the bleak Switzerland of our island cannot boast.

At some distance from Sazados we came to a strong pass, which might very easily be defended. Four forts have been thrown up on the commanding points: they cover the whole of the op-posite country, and the only practicable road to the river which runs at the foot of these mountains. In winter this water must be very formidable, as, from its situation amongst the hills, at that season of the year it becomes a most rapid and unstemable torrent. From the natural station of this position, a very few men could maintain it, and prevent the penetrating of any body of troops into this quarter of the kingdom.

Notwithstanding such an advantage, General Junot entered here; and no precaution having been taken by the country, he advanced unimpeded. In passing through a deep valley a little onward, he found the bridge of the river had been carried away by the violence of the waters. Not to be checked, he ordered a body of cavalry to swim the stream; but it was too potent for them: few accomplished their task, and upwards of two squadrons were drowned in the attempt.

The late summer having been particularly dry we met with no obstacle of this kind, the waters in most places being easily fordable. From their usually uncertain state, rendered so by sudden and deluging rains, the march of an army through the interior of this country is extremely precarious.

What added considerably to the sublimity of the way we had recently come, were the mists and clouds veiling; and occasionally discovering, by beautiful breaks, spots in the landscape of the most exquisite interest. After traversing a sort of undulating plain of hills, we rose upon Sazados, a village built on the summit of a romantic height, and embosomed in a wood of cork and chestnut trees,

At the entrance or end of these places there is generally a little building, wherein ought to be deposited the grain for its annual supply. Near it rise four or five large stone crosses, which make good objects; and when accompanied by a few natives lying in all the luxury of rags and indolence at their feet, the scene does not compose a bad picture.

Though so diffuse on the inanimate beauties of the country, I cannot pay a similar compliment to the living objects of attentions Our hosts were civil to us as we passed along; but their society afforded us neither interest nor amusement. Almost always, they had recourse to the guitar; and sometimes stunned us intolerably with their vocal accompaniments.

We left our little village at nine o'clock in the morning, under a most copious rain, which attended us the whole way till we reached Castello Branco, a distance of three leagues. Here, we found some insolence and unwillingness to oblige: but a little French military proceeding on our parts, soon brought the master of the mansion to his senses; and we made him produce whatever we had occasion for.

Owing to the wet weather it was next to an impossibility to walk much into the city: but what little I did see convinced me that it must be very ancient. The remains of a lofty castle, and long-extending towered walls, proclaim the consequence it once held in the kingdom of Portugal; and now stand splendid monuments of the architecture of former ages. The town is built on the side of a granite rock; which circumstance produced some odd effects in the interior, as many huge masses of the above-mentioned stone rose in immoveable obstinacy amidst the chapels and other buildings allotted, as quarters, to the British troops.

Our road, after leaving Castello Branco, was excellent; and the inclemency of the weather abating, we journeyed on in tolerable comfort. We passed over a fine bridge, evidently of a very antiquated age: but beautiful as such remains may be, the modern architecture of the Portuguese does not deserve less praise. Their tanks and fountains, so useful to the traveller, decorate the roads with every appropriate ornament of good taste and excellent workmanship.

The evening of this day brought us to Idanhia Nova. This place is built on a high rocky hill; and possesses the ruins of an old fortress which, over an extensive plain, commands a view of the Spanish mountains. Here, the country began to shew its own natural riches, and a specimen that the Portuguese can be industrious. Cattle, grain, and olives abounded; and from the latter an oil is pressed, not inferior to the Italian. In fact, we found every necessary of life in great plenty; and did not make a niggardly use of our good fortune. The inhabitants look much better than their neighbours, although dirt, and an indescribable appearance of misery, still mark them all to be of the same family. Was so luxuriant a soil in the hands of a more active people (for these acquire the name of industrious only by comparison), how valuable would this part of the country become to the state!

We now rapidly approach that country whose patriotism has aroused the admiration of England, and led our armies, with the ardour of a crusade, to the Spanish shores. I must confess that my heart beats high at the prospect of so soon being introduced to those brave sons of liberty, on whose countenances I expect to see the blaze of enthusiasm; and from whose energetic examples will shoot that chivalric fire so much needed to inflame the obstinate coolness of some of our too straightforward heroes. I do not mean too direct in the field, but too wedded to common-place modes. They understand not the glorious impulse which arms the undisciplined peasant; and makes him, though not a soldier, a dauntless champion of his country's rights. Spain is now one in heart and in soul; and while she thus makes herself the forlorn hope of Europe, it is the policy, as well as the honour, of every independent sovereignty to support her in so sublime a struggle. We go! and may heaven's propitious star crown our united efforts!

Mounted early in the morning for our long march, we descended a steep hill into the plain; and crossed the river Ponsul, which flows at the foot of this rugged mountain. The road is very good; and being shadowed by a dark wood for some distance, contrasted by its narrow glooms, the wide solitariness of the hills we had left. As we rose a commanding hill, and turned ourselves round, our eyes fell back upon our past footsteps, and we beheld a most extensive and sublime stretch of black mountains in the rear of our advancing army. The proud and alpine summit of the rock on which stands the fortress of Monta Santo, and the nearer heights, pierced the clouds; while far in the distance, the stupendous mountains in the vicinity of Guarda and Almada shrouded in snows, and flashing their silver radiance in the sun, seemed to cap their heads even in the azure sky.

On my rising early this morning, the view from the castle of Idanhia Nova was curious and beautiful. Clouds rolled in one white mass below on the plain; and from the bright light of the sun already up, the appearance was like a frozen sea covered with a northern snow. But when the heat took effect, the delusion evaporated; and the casual openings in this airy ocean presented the far distant country and mountains with all the visionary indistinctness, or glittering charms of enchantment.

Zibrira, where we stopped, intending the day following to pass the Spanish frontiers and halt at Alcantara, is a very small and dirty place, not containing more than 150 inhabitants. Here I saw children, rather too old for such exhibition, wandering about the village in groups totally naked. The women were better looking than any of the natives I had lately seen; and wore rich gold necklaces, and other ornaments. Their dress was nowhere else particular, unless I except the enormous bunch of petticoats that hung about them.

Tomorrow I hope to write from the Spanish dominions, and then you will have objects of greater interest.—*Adieu*!

LETTER 8

Alcantara, November 17th, 1808.

My Dear S——.

A continued hilly heath brought us to Zagura, the last Portuguese town on this route, previous to our entering Spain. It stands commandingly; possessing a fine old castle now in ruins. The Elga runs at the foot of the height on which the town is raised; and its stream is crossed by a bridge of ancient Roman date, presenting an object well worthy the pencil of the artist, and the admiration of the antiquary. Mouldering relics of all ages render this romantic river still more interesting. And single towers, the frontier posts of feudal times, at remote distances, stand in solitary grandeur on the bold precipices which embattle the waters.

After crossing the bridge we bade *adieu* to Portugal; and with the proud enthusiasm of Don Sebastian and his followers, when they leaped on the African shores,—entered Spain! But here, I trust, the resemblance will stop. We come to a friendly country; he went to a hostile one. We do not merely carry our own strength, but are to join hosts of determined patriots ready to fight or to die in defence of their injured land. How can we then, with such advantages, doubt of marking our track with victories; and, at the close, plant the united colours of England and of Spain upon the farthest promontory of the Pyrenees!

Five leagues brought us to Alcantara, and spread before us a sublime view of its great remains.

This place has long been one of the first consequence in Spain. It owes its origin and name to the splendid bridge of Trajan, which stretches across the Tagus; and in after timed it redoubled its celebrity by the knights which took their title from its

54

domains; and by its having heroically sustained two memorable sieges, in 1214 and 1706.

The Moors, when they were paramount in this country, were the first who established a residence here. They fortified their new city with ranges of strong walls and towers, and supported it with considerable force and magnificence. By what I observe, it appears as if the Romans did not find it requisite to maintain the passage of their superb bridge with more than a very slight guard. The guard-house, and a small temple on the town side of the bridge, are the only remains of a Roman settlement; and as the structure of their buildings is as invincible as were their arms, I have no doubt, had there been more habitations originally here, they would still be traced amongst the Moorish elevations.

This immortal proof of the greatness of Trajan's views—this unequalled bridge, consists of six arches, rising stupendously over the torrent They are erected on buttresses; and the stones are formed as was the usual Roman method, unhewn near the edges; a manner which not only provides against the destruction of time, but likewise gives a solid and bold air to the architecture.

The length of the bridge is upwards of six hundred feet, about twenty-nine broad, and two hundred high. These dimensions will give you some idea, though a faint one, of the grandeur of this gigantic work. On the centre of the bridge is an elevation, like a triumphant arch, under which the passenger must go in passing from one end to the other. In the middle of the arch is an inscription on a tablet, and on each side of it are others; two of which are scarcely discernible, though of a much more modern date than the former one. I have copied and enclosed that on the tablet, which is Trajan; and also another inscribed by Charles the Fifth, importing the repairs made by his orders. So far the detail: but no description can give an exact idea of the *coup d'œil* the whole scene presents.

The town is situated on a precipitous and rocky hill, close to the river. The approach from the Portuguese side is over a steep descent of shelving rocks, winding round a barren mountain. On a sudden the brown waters of the Tagus break upon the sight, swollen by the hundred, streams which sweep down the surrounding heights, and terminating in a rapid and roaring

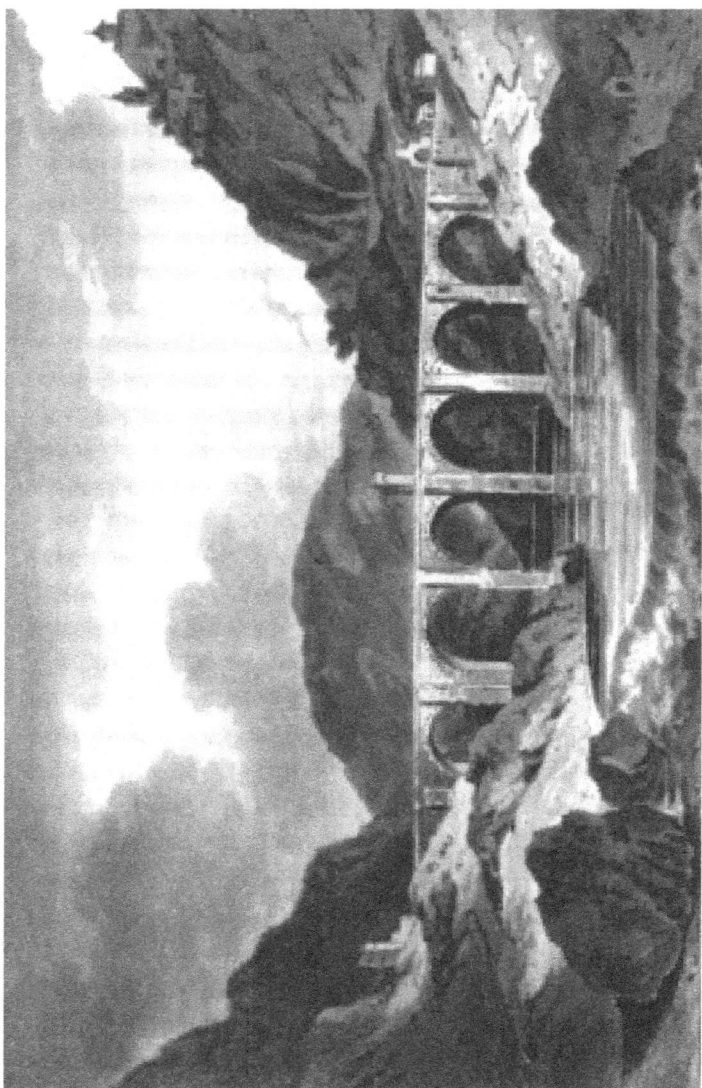

TRAJAN'S BRIDGE

cataract, about two hundred yards below the bridge. The city crowns the opposite mountain, and looks with dilapidated majesty on the time-defying structure of the once dictators of the world. Our, pleasure, on beholding so sublime a view, associated with the reception we expected to meet from the Spanish people, gave tenfold enjoyment to the delight with which we contemplated the proud walls of Alcantara. They seemed a type of the brave nation we came to defend; noble in ruins, and settled on the impregnable rock of nature, determined to maintain their existence against those attacks which shook other places to their foundation.

With such sentiments, such respect and cordiality for the inhabitants, did we enter Alcantara. But the governor proved a beast—a vulgar, uncivil animal, with little power to serve us, and less inclination. He was asleep when we called on him. Indeed all seemed asleep to the feelings we brought along with us. They received us with the coldness of men, shewing they were resolved ever to consider us as strangers, and treated us with, an inhospitality they durst not have ventured had they not believed us to be friends. We were wretchedly quartered; and the governor's excuse for this was, that he had no authority to force the people to receive us into more respectable houses.

The interior of the city is nasty; filled with crumbling walls, and churches in a desolate state. There appears to be a very extensive religious institution here, which possesses a fine Gothic structure, unfinished; and a noble cloister filled with many curious remains.

It may seem ridiculous, the observation I am now going to make, but it is impossible not to notice the object of it; namely, the number of pigs of prodigious fatness! They prowl about the streets in droves, seeking for that filth to which they owe their exuberant rotundity. Pork, therefore, is the beef and mutton of the people; and, as for milk, it is as difficult to procure as ice in the crater of Etna. Take the city all in all, for so large and apparently well populated a town, I could not have conceived it possible that so few absolute necessaries can be found.

Dirt reigns here with equal sway as in Portugal. And my expectations of receiving a comforter under these ills, from the civility of the people and their blazing enthusiasm, evaporating in the general coldness of the place, I could only ruminate within myself on the romantic fables we had heard, or the marvellous difference between the insensible inhabitants of Alcantara and their ardent brethren of the interior.

The specimen we meet here of the Spaniards gives them in countenance decidedly the superiority over the Portuguese. They are less in stature, but their faces have an air of intelligence and candour not generally possessed by their Lusitanian neighbours. And what increases their advantage is, the gay taste of their costume.

The females wear a sort of black cowl over their heads, hanging in long folds down their backs: short petticoats of all colours, with extremely pretty legs covered with red or black worsted stockings, terminated by leathern shoes and large silver buckles, complete the dress of this fair race. The males, like the Portuguese, are enveloped in brown cloaks, with large flapped hats; and, not to be behind them in loftiness of spirit, they never condescend to run the risk of being fatigued with any employment more active than idleness.

There are no regular Spanish troops in this place. The inhabitants mount guard at the governor's quarters. On our first route thither we met an officer and two patriotic dragoons, armed with long rusty swords, a solitary pistol, and, I believe, a carbine. Their rags and wretchedness peeping from under their threadbare mantles; and their uncouth manoeuvres, added to a sort of savage consequence arrogated by them on the cause of their becoming soldiers, gave them more the air of *banditti* than that of saviours of the state. Their horses were yet worse appointed, and seemed more unserviceable.

If these indolent, insolent Alcantarans be specimens of the army we are to join, I cannot augur a very brilliant campaign. What are half a dozen idle and vain fellows turning out in each city to do for the rescue of the whole kingdom? Nothing less than a universal spirit in the nation will be adequate to the great cause we have in hand. Nothing less than this universal spirit, did we expect would hail us! But at present faint are our hopes. We nowhere see that disinterested zeal amongst the nobles and the wealthy, which ought to pour forth their abundance on the loyal peasantry.

Nor do we meet the peasantry at every turn anything like the living originals of those animated descriptions we read in

England:—the higher classes devoting themselves to disciplining, clothing, and arming the lower; and the lower giving up every selfish consideration to the great end of freeing their country! Such a union alone can effect the present design of Spain. With such a zeal as this; with every heart and hand rising *en masse,* determined to accomplish the liberty of their country, or to find graves in her bosom; what may not ten millions of inhabitants achieve?

What a few undisciplined Asturians did against the reigning Moors in the eighth century, might not the collected people of Spain effect against a similar tyranny in the nineteenth? I am persuaded that in all cases of this kind there is nothing like unanimity and resolution. Look at the annals of the north, and see what the Dalecarlians have done for Sweden: cast your eye nearer home, and behold a handful of brave Scots driving the armies of Edward the First out of their country. Nay, look within your own land, and see a few valiant hearts on Runimede giving laws to a monarch leagued with many powerful states, and protected by the thunders of the Vatican!

A determined soul declares its high origin, that it partakes of divinity. There is something almost omnipotent in its will; secure of inward might, it "treads down impossibilities;" and mounts with resistless energy to the zenith of its hopes. Thus have been the resolves and the success of Bonaparte. And if such be the consequence of one man's determination, what may not be expected from the resolution of thousands when united as one! And then, if right brace the warrior's arm, will not the righteousness of the Spanish cause, when supported as it is, be more than sufficient to compel the ambitious star of usurpation to "pale its ineffectual fires?"

I have accompanied this letter with a sketch of the bridge, and of the archway which crowns its centre. The following is the inscription on the tablet which runs along its top.

INSCRIPTION OVER THE ARCH ON THE BRIDGE AT ALCANTARA.

Imp. Caesari. Divi. Nerva, F. Nervae
Traiano. Avg. Germ. Dacio. Pontif.
Max. Trib. Potes. VIII. Imp. Cos, V. P. P.

(To Caesar Imperator, son of divine Nerva, Nerva Traianus Germanicus Datius, Maximus Pontifex, Tribunita Potestas for the 8th time, *Imperium* for the 5th time, *pater* of the *Patria*.)

Carolus. v. imp. Caesar. Augustus.
Hispaniarumque. Rex. Hunc. Pontem.
bellis. etantiquitae. ex. parte. deruptum.
ruinam qui minatim in stauriius.
Sit, Anno domini. M. O. XLIII. Imperiius. VI. XXIIII.
Regni vero XXVI .

O IMP. NERVAE. TRAIANO.   Roman
te CAESARI. AVGVSTO. GERMANICO.
DACICO. SACRVM.
TEMPLVM. IN. RVPE. TAGI. SVPERIS.
ET. CAESARE. PLENVM. ARS.
VBI. MATERIA. VINCITVR. IPSA.
SVA. QVIS. QVALI. DEDERIT.
VOTO. FORTASSE. REQVIRET.
CVRA. JVVAT. INGENTEM. VASTA.
PONTEM. QVAM. MOLE. FECERIT.
SACRA. LITATVRO. FECIT. HONORE.
LACER. QVI. PONTEM. FECIT.
LACER. ET. NOVA. TEMPLA. DICAVIT.
ILLIC. SE. SOLVVNT. HIC. SIBI. VOTA. LITANT.
PONTEM. PERPETVI. MANSVRVM. VN. SAECVLA.
MVNDI.
FECIT. DIVINA. NOBILIS. ARTE LACER.
IDEM. ROMVLEIS TEMPLVM. CVM. CAESARE. DIVIS.
CONSTITVIT. FELIX. VTRAQVE. CAVSA. SACRI.
C. JVLIVS. LACER. H. S. I.
ET. DEDICAVIT. AMICO. CVRIO. LACONE. ICAEDITANO

After gratifying our antiquarian curiosity, nothing further excited our attention in, this once famous spot. Had the people answered our expectations, every object would have teemed with interest. But the soul was not there we hoped to find, the mere carcasses of Spaniards were not for us; and we turned from them with disgust and contempt. The major objects of our march being anywhere but at Alcantara, we in vain looked for the minor ones of comfort. The town, though full the size of any one of our most respectable provincial cities, contained neither an inn nor a coffee-house. The wretched hole whence post-horses are supplied may perhaps arrogate the title of one of these receptacles of mercenary hospitality; but in merit it deserves the name of shed, hovel; anything but that of a place habitable for human beings. That you may never shelter in the like, is the wish of your sincere, &c.

LETTER 9

Plasentia

We bade *adieu* to the city of the white bridge without any regret; and, I am happy to say, there left behind us most of those prejudices against the Spanish manner of supporting the patriot cause which that inhospitable place had occasioned.

The country over which we now travelled was highly dangerous for horses, on account of the rocky steepness of the road; and for carriages it was wholly impassable. At the distance of a league we again came upon the Tagus, whose foaming roar, long ere we reached its abrupt sides, apprised us of our near approach, Here, being to cross to the opposite bank, with great difficulty, and at different times, we embarked our horses and mules on a sort of square boat, which wafted us, or rather was violently driven by the impetus of the stream, to the point where we were to land.

Two leagues of savage waste marked the residue of our way till we arrived at a neat little village called Ceclavin. Nothing of the base parsimony and cold-blooded patriotism which disgraced the proud city of Alcantara was seen within these humble walls. We were kindly received by the chief man of the town. He was married, and, to the honour of his fair dame, his habitation possessed an air of greater regularity and comfort than we had seen in any house since our march. Soon after our arrival an excellent dinner was set on the table, at which both the lady and her spouse presided; partaking of its good things with more than common union, as they both eat off the same plate and drank out of the same cup.

After a dessert of grapes well preserved, and most hospitable libations of their juice, we were invited into the outer room, which was a kind of hall. There we found the whole village assembled and seated around, while a capacious pan of charcoal glowed in the midst of a circle of mats, so placed for the host and his friends. Fiddles, guitars, &c. finished the apparatus for the pleasures of the evening. The young ladies were dressed in their gala habits, and the men in their gayest attire. A dance, of course, seemed to threaten our patience.

The *bullero* was to be the exhibition. You already know its merits by my description of the like performance at the theatre in Lisbon. Speedily, therefore, the *Vestris* of the train rose; took out his lady; and the appropriate music striking up, produced a species of agility before us not very graceful, but most undoubtedly excessively droll. The female displayed great dexterity in keeping time, not only with the noise of her *castanets*, but with the silent movements of her bottom; which in elasticity far exceeded the quickness of her feet.

The *kosack*, and almost all the native dances of uncultured nations, and the *bullero* we must rank with these, were invented to express somewhat more than the tender passion: and certainly the one we have just been witnessing is not the most platonic of them all. Disgusting as it was to our eyes, the honest *Ceclaviners* liked it well; and a frequent repetition of the amusement took place during the evening. To change the scene a little, we commenced ballet-masters, and prevailed upon our village company to attempt an English country dance; in which they succeeded a *mervielle*.

The dress of the girls at this little fête was rather pretty in parts. They wore their hair in nets (the first of the sort I had seen), decorated with large bows of riband, whose ends hung flaunting down their backs. White handkerchiefs covered their shoulders; and a long and uncouth waist in stiff stays, rose from between a pair of hips branching out *a la hollandoise*. Their petticoats were very short; an apt fashion for displaying the beauty of their neat legs and feet. No want of gold was apparent here; as quantities of it formed into necklaces terminating in huge crosses, and massive ear-rings of the same gorgeous metal, shone upon their persons. The gayest colours, such as red, yellow, green, &c. were the general hues of their *habiliments*.

The ball ended at eleven o'clock: and refreshments in the form of wine, &c. flowed about most profusely. The *segar* too was not less used, as all the males present inhaled its somniferous perfume.

On retiring, we found clean and excellent beds, and slept soundly under the protection of a couple of bronze crucifixes that overhung our pillows.

This little village, I am told, is peopled with a horde of smugglers. And accordingly more contraband articles find their way in and out of its walls that pass through any other town in Spain. This sort of occult traffic is particularly lively between them and the English of the same commercial principles; and so for that reason perhaps, this fête was given to us in honour of our British smugglers. These gay villagers exhibited every appearance of comfort both in their habitations and themselves. Neither rags nor wretchedness were to be encountered here. All the rotundity of content, with the bloom of hilarity, marked not only the visages of the women, but of the men also.

Torrionsilla, at the distance of four leagues, was our next object. It is a village situated on a flattish hill, along which stretches forth an irregular line of poor-looking houses; but they are inhabited by a healthy and industrious people. Being the first British officers who had been seen in this place, we were presently surrounded like wild beasts at a fair; and had the pleasure of hearing that we were viewed with no inconsiderable degree of admiration. This was exemplified by more than words; for the *Avocat*, an agreeable and well-educated man, received us into his habitation, and treated us most hospitably.

The groups of women, whom we often pass at the fountains in this country, are beautifully interesting; their figures, dress, and dexterity in carrying water, are peculiar to themselves. The earthen vessel which contains it is of a simple form: and when placed upon the head, is in complete unison with their costume, and composes a picture worthy of the most tasteful pencil; reminding you of the celebrated work by Raphael, of the girl bearing the water vessel.

The Spanish nymphs seldom apply their hands to poise it, and will walk over the roughest ground without losing the balance.

The habitations of the peasantry consist of one storey and a ground floor; both are paved with brick; and the latter's windows are strongly barred with iron projecting into the street, which gives them the air of a range of prisons. The upper stories have nothing but wooden shutters; which, being kept open to admit the light, makes the residence as horribly cold in winter, as it is pleasantly cool in summer. The brick floors, too, add to these effects.

During our various sojourns at the several quarters in which we halted, the natives of every class and calling were admitted into our *refectories*; smoking, and staring at us whilst we eat, and between the whiffs asking ten thousand questions; besides exclaiming enthusiastically against the French and their emperor; and with equal ardour expressing their gratitude and friendship for England. And if physiognomy is to be believed, certainly we ought not to doubt the sincerity of this people; for, not only their aptness and activity, but their openness and vast superiority of mind over the Portuguese, give them ample claims for credits

Every league we advanced, after we left Alcantara, a vehement spirit of patriotism was professed by everyone. That ancient stumbling block of prejudice, the difference of religion, seemed totally buried; and the burning hatred which the Spaniard heretofore used to cherish against this heretics of Britons, was completely forgotten. Nothing was spoken of but the eternal amity which, from this period, is to subsist between the two nations: and even some went so far as to hope that such an honourable friendship may hereafter be sealed by an alliance between one of our royal females and their Ferdinand the Seventh. I had frequent opportunities of conversing on this and the like subjects with many of the best informed natives, a considerable number of whom were of the priesthood; and they one and all said, that the days of prejudice were past; that our conduct as a nation had proved more in favour of our creed, than a thousand volumes written to demonstrate its agreement with the gospel.

> And (continued they) if we need an additional argument to convince us in your behalf, have we not seen a nation of the same persuasion as ourselves, robbing, plundering, and depriving their brethren of their liberties; insulting the hallowed edifices they had solemnly sworn to venerate; and farther, to make a climax to their barbarous crimes, have they not added sacrilege to desolation? How then shall we estimate the true religion of

a people but by their actions? You are our protectors and friends; and, therefore, as the wounded Israelite said to the good Samaritan, we regard you as our neighbours and our brethren.

We left Torrionsilla at nine the following morning; and before the close of the day reached the valley of Plasentia; in whose bosom stands the fair city of that name, at a distance of six long leagues from the place whence we started. The road leading to this town is over a plain of great extent. On our approach vast piles of mountains rise to the view; their giant heads are crowned with snow, and look down proudly on the ancient walls of Plasentia. The valley is rich in vines, olives, and cypress trees, and receives a delightful interest from the meandering Xerte, which rolls its fertilizing waves through the scene. Numberless pale buildings and chapels rise from amidst the woods; and the venerable castle and tower, as well as the cathedral, present themselves in mouldering grandeur on the margin of the river, whose clear surface doubles these beauties by reflecting their forms. A noble stone bridge crosses the stream; its arches are modernised; but the whole bears evident marks of that era when a conquering people stamped their power by works of magnificence and utility. More Roman remains are to be met with in various parts of this bishopric; and as you know my fondness for the study, you will not be surprised that I should wish to halt a day, and have an opportunity of indulging in my favourite gratification.

(*In continuation.*)

Plasentia, Nov. 21.

I recommence my epistle, after having been busied in a very interesting way.

Our quarters are at the hotel of the Marquis de ———, a fabric of antiquated fashion, but undergoing a repair for the reception of His Excellency, now at Madrid. His superintendent received us with the greatest respect; and in our accommodations endeavoured to adopt everything to the English customs, as far as his knowledge would direct him.

But all civilities were not confined to him: we were visited by many of the most considerable inhabitants, amongst whom were the canons of the cathedral, who volunteered bringing us acquainted with everything worthy notice in the city. One, particularly loquacious, and possessing, or supposing he possessed, a deep intelligence in antiquities, held forth in Spanish on that subject most indefatigably; the more information he sought to give me, the nearer he approached my person; till at last the loudness of his voice, and the closeness of the contact, brought him to a recollection that I was not deaf, but only could not understand him. He, therefore, the following morning repeated his visit, attended by a brother *chanion*, who spoke French. I found him, on conversing with him, to be a man of erudition and knowledge of mankind. His mind was beautifully adorned by the most unprejudiced principles of religion and moral goodness. And, still more to brighten the picture, he possessed an elegant wit, and considerable musical talents.

Such an acquaintance was very desirable; and under his auspices we sallied forth to visit the curiosities of the city.

The cathedral was the first place we visited. Its exterior is of a bad mixture of Arabesque and Roman architecture, overloaded with ornament and clumsy columns. The interior is of perfect Gothic, with an altar composed of oaken sculpture, richly gilt and painted. This piece of workmanship must be at least three centuries old. Part of the edifice is yet unfinished; and at the uncompleted end stands the more ancient cathedral, of a pure taste, and most gloomily grand. I hope the want of means to decorate it in the proposed new fashion will long allow it to rear its reverend spires above the popinjays of modern architecture.

We next proceeded to the palace of the bishop; his lordship received us cordially, offering his house and all it could afford, even to his carriage, to our use during our stay at Plasentia, he expressed in the most sensible language his gratitude to the English nation for their exertions in favour of Spain; and hoped, that we would think his the voice of the *junta* of that province. Happening to admire a large picture of Saint Francis which hung near the Episcopal throne, he instantly begged our acceptance of it; of course we declined taking advantage of his generosity. Indeed, had we been in the least of spoiling dispositions, we might have come away well endowed from most of the places we visited; but we refused their presents, I hope not ungraciously: certainly it would have been base to have appropriated the overflowing gratitude of an already plundered people.

Having left the good bishop, we turned our steps towards the castle; but found it, though picturesque at a distance from its commanding situation, a mere shell within. As we passed on, we were invited by some Dominican monks into their monastery; when we entered, they all embraced us, and with equal energy of gesture and expression inveighed against the common enemy.

The holy brotherhood surrounded us on all sides; their various forms of young, old, fat and lean, presented groups truly novel and interesting. Having ascended the large staircase of the convent, we were ushered into a long and faintly lighted room, in which sat the abbot. Many of the elder brethren were likewise seated, being so many proofs of the good effects of holy seclusion, penitence, fasting, and other mortifications of the flesh.

The whole body of monks now furnished the apartment. Cakes, wine, and many good things were produced; the sparkling cup went rapidly round, and. gave new zest to toasts of our lasting amity and public friendship; these bursts of convivial enthusiasm were accompanied by embraces, and every act of pantomimic assurances of fellowship and love. In short our visit had more the appearance of some extravagant scene on the stage, than the sober converse of a society of holy men.

Just before we departed they conducted us into the refectory, which displayed every preparation for good. living. Eleven o'clock is their usual hour of dinner. During our walk home we visited an institution I was some little surprised at finding here: namely, a foundling hospital! On its being pointed out to me by one of our divine attendants, I exclaimed—"My God! what an *enfans trouvée* instituted in a town like this! It is the last place in the world I should have expected to have found one."

He laughingly replied, "What are those to do who dare not marry?"

The building is of considerable extent, appears clean, and is attended with much care. I do not doubt but that it is the human, *depôt* of the province.

We returned to the marquis's, to dinner; and after our hospitable meal, our good superintendent led us over the mansion to shew us the antiquities, and the splendour, of the house.

Amidst the numerous apartments, one vaulted saloon was filled with armour of all descriptions, both for horse and foot, besides swords, cross-bows, and chests filled with arrows. All are in a sad neglected state, and likely to remain so: for His Excellency finding no possibility of re-polishing them, has left them to rust; and perhaps, in the end, to be sold for old iron. Had we them in England, what a treasure would they be to our antiquarians! how nobly would they emblazon the halls of some of our new and unshielded *noblesse*!

He led us from the armoury to a sort of cloistered terrace; the walls of which were enriched with many a Roman fragment, found in the town and its neighbourhood. The relics thus preserved are altars, funeral stones, and one or two *basso relievos*. One, a boy squeezing grapes, is of very excellent sculpture. On a branch of the vine in this piece, is a bird, and a serpent winding up the stem: symbols I could not decipher.

Another, of equally good workmanship, is a figure placed in a sort of niche cut into the solid marble. It is a female gracefully covered with drapery, and sealed on a chair, bearing on her knee a basket of fruit; at her right side is a dog, and over her head the following inscription:

> DIIS MNIB
> ROMNAE INRIFINI
> VXORI OPIIM.

> D . M . S.
> AMMONMXRA
> AN. XVIII. AMMO
> NICVS. MAVRVS
> FILIAE. PIBNTIS
> SIMAE. F.

The *basso relievo* of the boy is fixed on a tablet, on which is engraven an accompanying inscription.

> MHTHP · MOI · ΓΑΙΗΝΑ
> ΠΑΡΗΡΙΟΝΟΟΤΙΟΟΔΟΤε
> ΗΓεΠεΟΤΗΑΗΝΟΤΝΠΑΤΙ
> ΟΦΟΟΝεΙΠΟΜΟΔΟΦΥΙ

> ΜΕΝΟΙΜΙΑΡΦΙεΠΙΗΝΓΑΡεΜΟ
> Μ ' : εΡΛΟΜΟΟΟΥΠΑΝΡΙΟΟΥ.
> NOMIOTAIANOC
> NOMINE. IVILIANVS. MENSESEX.
> DERRSEPTIM·HAVПICITVM·MVI
> ―――――――――――――――――――
> VM. ΗLEVII. VIERQVII. PARENS.

A mutilated bust of Antoninus, and two colossal heads in no better preservation, as well as many antique fragments of which I send you sketches, adorn this colonnaded repository. A very large foot, sculptured in the purest marble, at least four times the size of life, next caught our attention, it is covered by a richly decorated sandal, worthy indeed of the first artist of the classic age in which it was hewn. The figure to which it has been attached must have been immense; and from the fashion of the sandal, I have hardly a doubt that it was the statue of some warrior.

We closed the evening of this day at the house of our *chanion*. He had not only attentively conducted us through the city, but had prepared a little concert for us, that we might part, in every way, harmoniously. The Adonis or *Mercutio* of the town played and sung to his guitar with all the affectation of a finished coxcomb. And I am positive, the subject of the airs he chanted must have far out-stepped the bounds of decency, as the Spanish part of our society seemed to enjoy them most potently; their countenances betraying a rather sensual demonstration that love and its consequences were the burthen of these verses.

On our return to our quarters we found that his grace the bishop had been to visit us; leaving two turkeys and as many bottles of rum for our supper. The latter present arose from an idea that the English cannot finish the day without punch. Fearing that you will think I never will finish this letter I remain, &c.

LETTER 10

Salamanca, November 26th, 1809.

Dear S———.

We separated in my last at Plasentia; which city saw us depart the succeeding morning to that in which we halted; and very deeply impressed were we with the kindness of the inhabitants,

On our issuing forth, our two clerical friends were at the door of the marquis's hotel to bid us *adieu*; and our parting, I assure you, was not a little pathetic—much friendship was avowed on both sides; and their last words were prayers for our, success and health.

I never beheld a more beautiful morning; but that is nothing strange with the inhabitants of this favoured city:—bland are the people, and bland is their climate. I am told that the air around this delightful spot is almost always serene and heavenly. Though now far advanced in the month of November, nothing but the name of that ungenial season is known here. The softest air of the sweetest summer day could not be more balmy than that which met our freshened senses on turning out for the march. The sun shone in full power; and its bright beams, while they warmed the bosom of the hill we were to ascend, glittered on the cold snows of the yet more distant heights, we were also destined to cross.

We left the town by a road near to the castled ruins. It had been a Roman way; was broad, and paved with regularity. Adjoining the outward gate rises an aqueduct of the same era with the road, and consisting of fifty arches, which cover a vast extent of ground, and form a grand variety, when thus opposed to the black towers of Plasentia.

The view of the city on this quarter is not so magnificent as the one on our approach. It wants the lofty heights rising directly above its walls, and the aspiring icy heads of the mountains afar off: but though inferior to the absolute perfection of the sublime on the other side, yet all was so admirable here, that we quitted the romantic involvements of the antique and vineyard-clad road with regret, and soon lost sight of the ever-respected environs of Plasentia.

Our route lay in a direct line to the tracks of distant snow; however we speeded on, and before many hours passed away, found ourselves entirely out of the temperate zone, and introduced to the circles of extreme cold and misery. A march of six leagues brought us to a village called Aldea Nueva; and as it lay in the midst of snow, and the inhabitants seemed frozen alike with cold and indolence, no wonder, when fresh from the warm comforts of Plasentia, that we should ill brook the penury of our present reception. However the metropolitan turkeys saved us from actual want in this instance; and glad were we in the morning when the signal was made for our march.

Having dispatched our domestics betimes in the advance, we followed when the sun had obtained a little power, and continued our course along the brow of this freezing district. After a few hours patient endurance of the bitter blast and driving snow, we descended the mountain; and, as a reward for our brave sufferance of such ills, got into a rich valley, whose autumnal warm tints was a pleasing change from the laid pale monotony of the scene. The road in many parts still exhibited curious remains of Roman industry and greatness. Many a mile of well-paved causeway pointed out to us the footsteps of the emperors of the world.

Ah! my friend, how many *memento mori* were here of the transitoriness of all human power? The ruins of bridges crossing the dry beds of once rapid streams; the cylindrical stones which marked the military distances, were yet unbroken: but what are the divisions they were intended to limit?—where the hands which planted them? Let our modern Caesars of the earth view these relics, and lay to heart the emptiness of all conquests that is not over vice; the faithlessness of monuments which outlive the names they were planted to immortalize! These stones stand; but their inscriptions are almost totally worn out by time. Having so lately left the scorching suns of Lisbon, and the more delightful atmosphere of Plasentia, you will not be surprised that we should find these snow-clad regions insufferably cold. Even this valley, which was somewhat more tolerable than the heights, was rendered indescribably chill by the blasts from the fountains. Perhaps you will scarcely credit it, that at Aldea Nueva we felt eight degrees of frost.

Not any of us being apprised that we should encounter such severity. I fear that all the officers are in a similar predicament with myself; and I have not brought an article of warm clothing with me. As to the poor soldiers, they stand a good chance of being transformed into moving icicles, in marching from quarter to quarter. A few of your benevolent ladies' flannel jackets would be of use here. Indeed (ignoramuses that we were, not better to inform ourselves) we did not harbour a thought that in a country so famous for glowing suns we could ever experience such hyperborean blasts.

In the last village we stopped at, our horses, mules, &c. being quartered at the inn, I paid it a visit, being curious to see what were the comforts accessible to travellers who bad not the advantage of claiming military lodgings. I put my head into this ark for man and beast, and found it a most forlorn, dark, dirty hole. One large unpaved room, without even a window, formed the main saloon of the hotel. A sort of recess at one end, where burnt a wood fire (whose light but more gloomily shewed the darkness of the superior apartment), seemed like the obscure haunt of sorcerers or *banditti*. Around this hearth sit the guests and family, open to the intrusions of every boor whom curiosity or necessity may lead to make one in the circle.

If by accident a traveller have not his own bedding, a wretched nook is his destiny, and a wooden bench; or, perhaps, if he is to be more highly favoured, he is thrust into a noisome hole, with a window open to the nocturnal roarings of the storm, and furnished with a rotten tester, straw mattress, and filthy sheets, well warmed with vermin of every species. A dusty brass crucifix protects the slumberer; while a cork-stool completes the furniture of an apartment, which the Spaniards think is adequately fitted up for any rank. To this then are all exposed who voyage it in so terrible a country! None are exempt from tasting its miseries but we sons of the sword; and therefore, bad as our present quarters were, a comparison with this blessed hotel made us fancy ourselves in paradise.

Fuenta Olio is four, leagues from Aldea Nueva, Its first appearance did not promise very fair; but the respectable air of the church inspired us with a hope that its pastor might be a man of more entertaining means than his flock; so, without troubling the chief magistrate of the place, we made directly for his holiness's abode. Our judgement was good. The clergyman received us with hospitality and enthusiasm. He had two nieces in the house who acted as domestics: they were very pretty, and by no means bashful. We found likewise the wife of the village Esculapius, handsome and young; what in England we call buxom: more than could be said of her spouse; who was old, withered, and emaciated; the very picture of the apothecary in Romeo and Juliet.

The lady was by no means ignorant of her lord's imperfections; and a jolly friar, who we found on a visit to our priest, and to whom she doubtless had confessed her quick-sightedness, seemed to be to her both doctor and apothecary. This holy brother (who was so good a friar in things terrestrial as well as celestial, as to be eager for fraternity in all) to amuse us danced the *bullero* with great execution and gesture, tucking up his saintly drapery around his waist, and displaying a pair of strong limbs in leather breaches, which he used with much motion and agility. The married dame assisted at this pastime; which certainly more became the drunken revels of a boorish fair than the sober chamber of a Christian minister.

From this instance, you will see that the merry legends of monkish jollity are not to be doubted. Were I to let you into all the secrets which this dancing son of the church whispered into our ears, you would never more hesitate to believe that Comus and his crew tire often the reigning deities in Spanish monasteries; and I shall never again express my wonder should I see an *enfans trouvée* at the door of every convent in the kingdom. Indeed our liberal friar seemed so overflowing with the goods of the village, that he was put backward in his wishes that we should share not only the hospitalities of the benevolent pastor, but even the beds of his nieces, and the wife of the surgeon barber.

After thanking our hosts for all their kindnesses, at ten the following morning we took our leave. We passed through a thick mist as we descended rapidly into a plain of great extent, having on our right a high and stupendous range of snowy mountains, whose heads pierced the sea of clouds that rolled before, above, and beneath us.

As the vapour disappeared we had an opportunity of remarking the face of the country. Cultivation spread on every side; and forests of *lignum vitae* covered the sloping descents, leaving openings in the shade for corn, pasture, and other husbandry. Numerous herds of black cattle graced on the heights which hung over the valley of San Pedro; the spot destined for our next resting place.

At this part of the country the male peasantry's dress fully equalled the expectations of their costume with which I had entered Spain. They wear caps of the same form to which heralds give the title of cap of maintenance; their jackets are of the old fashion, with laces, tags, and slash sleeves, their feet and part of their legs are clothed in sandals; broad leathern belts girt their loins: in fact, take anyone of them so clad, and you see exactly the original actors in *Don Quixote* and *Gil Blas*.

At San Pedro we left one of the cleanest cottages I ever beheld. Such a thing is pleasant in any country; but here it is a rarity and a treasure. After bidding it a wistful *adieu*, we took our route by a very disagreeable road for near four leagues; but at length the high spires of Salamanca rose before us in Gothic majesty, and seemed to welcome us to a more prolonged and comfortable rest. Several soldiers whom we met told us that the greater part of our army were already assembled there, and hence we did not doubt of a little necessary halting time.

The appearance of the city at a distance is fine in itself, but the approach is unpicturesque, the surrounding country being bleak and treeless. A bridge of beautiful architecture thrown over the Tormes, leads to this little capital.

Here are we then safely arrived and in quarters. Being about to sally forth, not in search of adventures, but of information respecting the curiosities of this once famous place, I bid you a temporary farewell.

LETTER 11

Salamanca, November, 1808.

Alas, my good friend, Salamanca is like to prove as too long place of sojourn, I will not say of rest, to us all! We are too anxious, to find any repose in these quarters. But to proceed regularly.

Of course the length of time we were on our march prevented our receiving due information of what was doing around us, and certainly kept us in total ignorance of what was going on at home. We could form no other idea of what we were to meet here, but that we were to find thousands of brave Spaniards-in-arms, and our own troops ready to assist them. But now, having arrived at head-quarters, how are the pinions of my far-stretching expectations shortened! Some sad indecision seems to reign where it can least be pardoned; amongst the leading patriots of Spain.

We are totally ignorant of the plans of the Spanish generals; whether they mean to come to a junction with us, or to remain at a distance, yet rests within their own bosoms. I know, that before we came nothing regular on this score had been arranged between the two nations; although Lord William Bentinck had been (previous to any movement on our part) dispatched to Madrid to regulate the joint dispositions of ourselves and our patriotic allies; as well as to prepare the means of subsisting our army when it should march into Spain. Why this, march was so long deferred you best know at home; but I sincerely hope that the time we have passed at Lisbon since the Cintra convention may not be hereafter wished for here!

It was not, I believe, until the beginning of October that Sir John Moore received his appointment to the command of the troops then at Lisbon, and destined for this service. I understand that with you it was fully determined the north of Spain should be the point of rendezvous for our army, leaving the plans for its action to be settled as future circumstances, and the judgement of the Spanish commanders, with that of General Moore, should deem advisable. Our force being the auxiliary one, will, of course, when the chief command of the Spanish troops is disposed of, act according to the orders of the then grand leader.

I have been informed, however, that a plan had been formed at home respecting what was to be done provided the French did not advance with their usual rapidity. We were to join Blake and the Estramadura army, supported by the Portuguese; and to proceed towards the north, penetrating to the pass of the Pyrenees: whilst the central and southern armies were to advance and oppose the enemy in their quarter. During these movements Sir John Stuart was to be on the alert in Sicily, and render every assistance to our Spanish campaign, by the application of a British force in Catalonia.

In order to give you an idea of the state of the French and Spaniards in arms, before we began our march from Lisbon, I enclose you a list of their respective strengths. In compliment to our allies I shall begin with the Spanish armies.

Blake's army (since defeated, and which was to have been ceded to the command of the Marquis de la Romana, on that nobleman's arrival at its quarters) occupied Bilboa, Frias, Trespaderne, and Ordunna; and amounted to 30,000 men.

Romana (who was expected to disembark at Corunna, but who landed at Sant Ander), with 10,000 men, makes the left of the Spanish grand army about 40,000 strong. This force, we are told, was well appointed with artillery: but independent of Romana's 10,000, there are not more than 12,000 regulars in the whole division; all the rest being armed peasants.

Castanos commands the army of the centre, occupying Madrid, and extending to Soria, being 25,000 men, with upwards of forty pieces of cannon.

The army of Estramadura were then on their march to take up a position beyond Burgos. They were under the command of General Galluzo, and consisted of 12,000 men, the greater part of whom are formed into excellent troops; and are intended to become a line of communication between Blake and Castanos.

The army of Castile, headed by general Cuesta, at Burgo del Osma, comprises 12,000 men.

The army of Valencia, commanded by General Damas, at Barja, Tarazona, and Aguda, consists of 16,000.

The army of Catalonia is blockading Barcelona, and stretches in advance towards the French frontier; being, in all, about 20,000 men.

Several smaller corps are on their march from Arragon and Granada. And, from this computation we may gather, that the whole known military force of Spain with which we are to co-operate amounts to 141,000 men.

Our own force, when joined to General Baird (who now lies between us and Corunna), will not exceed 40,000. Surely, if these numbers were moved by one head (for unity of plan is indispensable when opposed to the military policy of Bonaparte), and if possessed by the enthusiasm which we are led to believe animates the Spanish nation, and we know inspires our own, surely with such an army, so well appointed in body and spirit, much might have been, and may yet be done. The soldier who determines to conquer has already won half the battle. And with nearly 200,000 men so resolved, and its vicinity, in order to keep up a communication with the centre. Being nearly annihilated, and their remains flying to Oranda, the enemy found free passage, and spread on all sides.

By similar misfortunes the whole Spanish army in this quarter, save Romana's, is defeated and dispersed; so that now our situation is very critical. Indeed difficult will be the task of our commander to decide on our next movement, as little hope can now be entertained of our forming the intended junction with Sir David Baird. Under the circumstances we are in, we cannot advance against the enemy until General Hope arrives with the artillery and cavalry. The country in our front is one continued plain, extending nearly to Burgos; so that should the French come up with us here in any force, we must do what is so repugnant to Englishmen, make a retrograde motion, and fall back upon the strong holds of Portugal. But in such a case, what will become of our right column?—I do not like to think upon it.

At present, our hopes are these—that General Hope will pass through Madrid on the 22nd of this month; and, of course, we devoutly pray that nothing may prevent his arrival at our quarters, as we have no cavalry with us, and only one brigade of artillery. Besides our military chest is with the absent column. You will naturally be astonished at the road this latter division of our army has taken; but it arose from the information we received from the Spanish military.—When we applied to them for the best route of march to the place of rendezvous they said that the artillery and cavalry could not advance by the road which was proper for our infantry to take; we therefore divided; and hence you see into what a dilemma we have fallen.

We are not only rendered incapable of withstanding the enemy, should he confront us with any body of troops, but we are tormented with the cruellest anxieties; and besides, have most undoubtedly (if there be anything yet in the plan of proceeding to Burgos) lost much time in waiting a junction with our cavalry. Whilst we are thus situated, I fear our adversary is not following our example; and that our present enforced rest will be aroused by the noise of still greater misfortunes.

In the midst of these disagreeables, it is some satisfaction to look upon the state of our army. You have no idea of its high order. The long march seems to have had no other effect on our men but to raise their spirits, and to make them more eager to come up with the foe. Were their numbers but doubled, and had we 7,000 or 8,000 cavalry in addition, we might then defy treble the number of French. But without cavalry, I repeat, we can do nothing on these vast plains.—So much are we prisoners, by this unfortunate advice of the Spaniards, that we cannot proceed a step; and should the enemy be still farther victorious (for they will now advance upon Castanos), their patrols may insult us, almost to the gates of Salamanca.

Had we Lord Paget with us at the head of only 2,000 or 3,000 British dragoons, I think a change in our present halt would instantly be adopted. As it is, we are fixed.

I am sorry to say that information respecting the military

movements nearer the capital is very difficult to be obtained; and when it does arrive, you cannot be at all certain that it is true. The most absurd reports are circulated, which bewilder the brains of the inhabitants, and sometimes are very likely to mislead us. Were we to judge of the able dispositions on this head by the number of couriers arriving and dispatched, we should suppose that a vast routine of business was carrying on; and that it would be impossible for the senders of them to be ignorant on any of the public affairs.—But by our experience of all this bustle, I have reason to fear that they bear, backwards and forwards, nothing more satisfactory than a train of questions, the result of which the French will finally answer; as they argue much indecision and discussion between this *junta* and the central one. Hoping my next may breathe fairer prospects, I remain your sincere, &c.

LETTER 12

Salamanca, Nov. 1808.

My last was on military matters: being in those respects just as we were, I shall change to a more promising subject, and describe the beauties, ancient and modern, of Salamanca. The city is extensive, containing at least 8,000 well-built houses, besides numerous monasteries, several elegant colleges, and splendid churches,—The cathedral, considered one of the finest in Spain, is a magnificent structure, but ornamented with ridiculous profusion. The west front is crowded with *basso relievos,* and grotesque figures of every kind, intermixed with saintly legends and the fanciful twinings of the vegetable world. The latter decoration is often adopted to supply the barren invention of the architect.

The interior of this holy structure is much superior to its exterior. It is simply ornamented, being of the latest and best style of Gothic; and is more admirable in this sober garb, than were it overcharged with the labyrinth of rich work so commonly introduced in similar buildings. This bad taste injures the harmony of the scene; destroying the fine religious gloom of its vaulted passages, lofty columns, and well-ceiled roof:-but modern affectation and ignorance never foil to ruin these beautiful specimens of antiquity by foolish additions and absurd amendments. Notwithstanding that, in part, this noble church of Salamanca has escaped such fopperies, yet there is sufficient done by the hands of these mistaken reformers sensibly to injure the whole.

Some years ago its old spire fell; and, woeful to relate, a sort of dome supplies its place, finely fretted and pilastered within, and decorated at all points and corners with every gay colour, besides silver and gold, in a most abominable Greek-Dutch taste.—Such is the crown now placed on the fine and graceful summits of the Gothic arches. The body of the church has suffered in like manner; the choir being enclosed by a similar effort of perverted skill. Were we to separate these two modern works from the cathedral to which they are attached, we might admire their ingenuity; but when applied as they are, the only sentiment they excite is disgust.

Several small chapels in the aisles are enriched with good paintings, carvings, monuments, and other commemorations of our Saviour and the saints. A picture of Leonardi di Vinci, representing the Virgin and the infant Jesus, and executed in his best style, is in one of them. In another chapel, over an altar, is a delightful performance: the entombing of Christ; large, and in exquisite condition; full of beauty, fine colour, and worthy the Venetian school. I should suppose it a Titian—at any rate it would do honour to his pencil when even in the zenith of its power.

So much for the works of art in this sacred building. I intend going to mass soon, that I may also behold those of nature in the beauty of the fair devotees.

A vast range of walls and towers surround the town. On these embattled ruins many houses are erected, whose elevated situation, architecture, and grated windows, together with the enriched spires of the religious buildings shooting up behind the city, give it, to the approaching traveller, more the appearance of an eastern capital than of a town in the little kingdom of Leon.

The bridge, which I have before mentioned, is of many arches; one half of the erection is Roman, and the other modern; but both are of great beauty. The city is built on an extensive plain; bleak, and almost treeless: nothing breaks the cheerless monotony, excepting here and there a village, until the eye meets the horizon hemmed in by huge mountains shrouded with snow. What I have yet seen of the inhabitants does not awaken in me any very glowing idea of their charms. They seem cold and insipid as their landscapes. The nobles dress wretchedly; the females without taste, and no trace of a national costume; being equipped in bad imitation of what the French wore twenty years ago. Waists extremely long, and thinly moulded, measure half the length of their persons (their stature being short); and thus destroying all symmetry, transform the female form divine into that of some nondescript ugly animal. However, if the middle be reduced to a mere nothing in point of thickness, the ladies of all ranks, high and low, make up for the deficiency in another part of their persona. Whether it be natural or artificial I cannot pretend to determine; but certainly that point of their fair bodies Which makes such active exertions in the *fandango* and *bullero* is most monstrously prodigious.

The men (I mean the *hidalgos* or gentlemen) are continually involved in their mantles; under which they wear a sort of German great coat. A coloured silk handkerchief binds their neck; and every mark of indolence, dirt, and absence of water, attends them.

I paid a visit the other evening to the house of the Marquis of ————, where I found several females, but not one of them possessed anything to interest. A little dance, with some music, assisted to enliven the hours which are passed without conversation or refreshment. In one corner of a large saloon sat a group of well-dressed *donnas*; in another, a similar assemblage of *dons*, Both parties encircled a sort of copper soup-dish, filled high with the embers of suffocating charcoal: the only means the natives have of heating themselves or their apartments. It may be agreeable to them, as *use doth breed a nature in a man*; but if never fails to give strangers a headache.

This was my first taste of Spanish society (for the honest folk who entertained us on our march are not to be honoured with so high a title!); and really I found it so stupid, so devoid of female graces on the part of the ladies, and of rational converse on the side of the men, that I have no wish to make a second attempt.

The next day I visited the Irish convent, anciently that of the Jesuits. It is of large extent; and in some of its quadrangles affords quarters for two of our regiments. The Irish attached to its establishment do not at present amount to more than twelve or thirteen; and yet it bears their name. Hence, I suppose the other colleges are not in a more flourishing state with regard to members In one quarter of the building is a magnificent cloister, protected by windows from the open air. Around this gallery, if so it may be called, are a series of pictures representing the principal events in the life of Ignatius; executed, I should think, by Bouchardon. They are respectably done, and preserved with great care; the cloister itself is of a beautiful modern architecture.

The hall of argument is extremely large, and not uninteresting; for at each end are portraits, though badly painted, of the ancient professors and most celebrated members.

This edifice is a grand monument of the power and consequence the Jesuits once possessed in this kingdom; and is not less a memorial of the magnanimity of his catholic majesty, who durst venture to issue the edict of their banishment. The secrecy and decision with which the act was performed is wonderful, and reflects immortal honour on the firmness of the king. In the March of 1767 did this memorable expulsion take place.

The power of these holy institutions seems rapidly decreasing; and as the people become enlightened and discover their absurdity which, should they continue their enthusiastic fellowship with the English they are likely the sooner to perceive, we may expect that the monasteries of Spain will gradually follow the fate of those in England and bespread the ground with their hallowed ruins. Indeed the brotherhoods and sisterhoods of these tombs of the living, already lose the reverence with the people which they once possessed: and from what I can observe, I do not believe the country at large would regret if every one of them were abolished at once. I could, and I will, send you, in some of my idle moments, a few anecdotes of these tender sisterhoods and of our troops, which happened during our march through the principal towns. At present I will return to graver matter.

In passing one of the churches the other day I heard a doleful chant issue from its door. I entered, and found a train of monks saying mass for the soul of a departed lady who lay like a waxen image extended before them on a black bier enveloped in a pall. Innumerable candles blazed around the corpse; and a solemn assembly of Carthusian fathers sung the service for the deceased, whilst several priests in embroidered vestments executed the sacred masses. These parts of the ceremony were very tedious; but I was resolved to see the last act that was to hide her, who had once been animated, admired, and loved, forever from the world.

Nothing could appear more like wax than she did; her hands met across her breast, and a golden crucifix sanctified them. At her feet stood her own female servant, praying continually, and counting her beads; also occasionally putting out and lighting a little taper. After a considerable time past in prayers and singing, a huge black crucifix was placed by a monk at the head of the grave (which was near an altar), then open to receive the deceased. A ragged, hairy-headed Spaniard, who, I suppose, was the grave-digger, walked up to the bier where the lady lay, and without feeling or decency took her up in his arms; raising her rather high in the air, and carried her thus awkwardly and indelicately to the grave. This group had a most extraordinary effect both to the eye and feelings. The contrast is not to be described; and the little ceremony used in the act added still more to my surprise and horror.

The coffin had been previously placed in the cenotaph of death, into which the man and his sacred burthen descended; he laid the lady into her narrow shell, at which instant four monks advanced with a black pall, and covered both from our view. What the man was about he and they best know: whether strewing quick lime on the corpse, or rifling it of the golden crucifix, &c. I cannot tell, but full ten long and silent minutes was he thus hidden in the grave with the dead body in question.

This part of his office finished, he pushed his rough hand from beneath the sable covering, and drawing from aloft the coffin-lid with his shovel, which lay at the side of the grave, he soon showered down the earth, and the enshrouded matron was seen no more. An anthem finished the ceremony. The procession of religious retired, preceded by the dark cross, and chanting a deep and melancholy air; while two huge bassoons, groaning in horrid concert, most dismally closed the scene.

I could not help remarking the little feeling, either of regret or of decency, which was exhibited in almost all present; as smiles and conversation amused them during what ought to have been considered the most awful of ceremonies.

This church, like all others in Portugal, is decorate with figures of Christ, the Virgin, and numberless hallowed personages. But it is not in the simple garb of holiness we see these images: they are attired in the most *outré* habits. The blessed mother being generally dressed in a sack and petticoat of rich brocade, with an elegant stomacher gorgeously beset with precious stones. Her arms are appendaged by long lace ruffles; and her head also most lavishly adorned with gold and tinselled glory.

The infant Jesus is not less absurdly accoutred; the whole forming a group more ridiculous than venerable. The Virgin is commonly placed on a very large half-moon: perhaps a similar emblem with the cross which rises over the crescent on the minarets at Moscow, being a figurative memorial of the triumph of Christianity over Islamism. At present the appearance of a female figure so united with the *lunal* planet cannot but remind one of the Astarte of the eastern idolaters, and her not uncommon appellation of Queen of Heaven renders the resemblance more striking.

Writing to you who have never seen the like, it is not easy to describe the effect which this strange assemblage of divine, heathen, and grotesque images make upon the mind on entering one of their temples. Indeed, while moved to laughter by their strange *habiliments*, I cannot view such a direct breach of our commandments, and such caricaturing of the most sacred subjects, without a degree of pain that is inexpressible. And as an instance how much these exhibitions are at war with all sober thought, I must describe to you one that caused a risibility in me, even till I was ashamed of myself. Indeed I defy the most marble-faced stranger from Britain to cast his eyes on it, and not to laugh immoderately. I mean a representation of our Saviour extended upon the cross. It is carved in wood, and as large as life; painted with great care, to portray the natural colour of the divine sufferer: and if this were all, it would be impossible to regard it without the most sublime feelings. But when the hand of absurdity has bound its loins with a white satin petticoat, richly embroidered, and finished with a deep gold fringe, the contrast between the figure and the dress, and the ridiculous effect of this odd mixture, is so surprisingly droll, that gravity must forget itself before such absurdity, and burst into a violent peal of laughter.

When compared with the Latin, the Greek churches certainly stand pre-eminent in solemnity, both of outward and inward decoration. And their religious ceremonies in no respect violate the seriousness of the truly devout. Their church displays no object that can deprive religion of her attendant awe; nor do the sacred rites present any farcical exhibitions that might give rise to ludicrous remarks or fastidious ridicule.

Another circumstance strikes the eye in the Spanish churches, which also gives birth to something more than a smile:—the dedication of waxen imitations of different parts of the body to the saints of the various shrines I should any unfortunate mortal have a lame shoulder, mutilated nose, humped back, or any other defect, he gets the affected part modelled in wax, and with a suite of prayers and sanctities, hangs it up amongst the canopied decorations of his favourite saint. And this is done in the hope that the canonized king's intercessions with the divine dispenser of pains and restoration will speedily make perfect his damaged frame.

You have no idea what strings of odd parts of the human person are here suspended in the shrines of the miracle-working saints. They say that a French commander collected sufficient of these waxen memorandums to keep him in candles the whole of his residence in Spain. This custom, nonsensical as it is, may boast a high antiquity. We may trace dedications of this sort, to propitiate the mediation of subordinate deities, both in the Greek and Roman rites of heathenism. But those offerings were generally on a grander scale and for mightier purposes; not for the advantage of one individual, but for the relief of thousands. So much for spiritual interests! I must lead you to consider our present temporal prospects in my next. Meanwhile *adieu*!

LETTER 13

Salamanca, November ——, 1808.

My Dear S——.

Did we live in the days of witchcraft, surely Napoleon would lose all his titles in that of sorcerer! It seems as if we were spellbound, and shut up by the magic seal of this Gallic Mahommed within the walls of Salamanca without power to do anything but to wonder at our fate.

Victorious in Portugal; waved on by enthusiasm herself to lock the outward gate of Spain against the flying enemy; marched into the very heart of the kingdom; where are now our triumphs, where the promised patriots in arms? All we expected to meet have made themselves air! The voice that summoned us is silent; the country is filled with a conquering foe; the Spanish armies are dispersed; and we find ourselves in a snare! Whithersoever we turn rumour brandishes the scythe that is to mow down our withering laurels, and perhaps our ranks into the bargain.

In fact, my dear S——, a terrible report is in circulation, that Castanos, who commands the only Spanish force of any strength, has been defeated! If this be true, our destiny must soon be decided; and, I fear, retreat, will be inevitable. There is no end, no limit, measure, bound, in that word is death to us all: it cuts off all our hopes; it robs us of our promised honours; and returns us to our country crest-fallen and broken-hearted. Happen what will, I am sure it is a word that our gallant commander will never bring himself to pronounce. In extremity, to retreat is indeed the hardest duty of the brave.

Some days ago the following statement was said to be the position of Castanos and Palafox. They occupied Alagon; stretching along the Ebro a force consisting of nearly 50,000 men. Several thousands of this army were peasantry, forming a communication with those in arms to the south, as far as the shores of the Mediterranean, Our prospect in front, you will perceive, is not improved since I last sketched its aspect. But not so the French; after beating Blake and the Estramadura corps, they possessed themselves of Burgos, and pushed their advantages in every part of the country.

I cannot guess what effect the defeat of Castanos (if true) will have on the people of this province. If they ever did sympathise with the patriotic declaration which brought us hither, they seem to have exhausted all their zeal before our arrival; for not a trace can we find of any interest in the cause: and when you look at their stupid indifference to public proceedings, you can hardly believe that this was the once formidable kingdom of Leon that swept the coasts of Spain clear from the usurpation of the infidels. The supineness of the inhabitants of this town is particularly detestable. So many brave Foreigners appearing in arms for the Spanish cause, we should naturally suppose would excite some degree of public spirit in the people; but far from it; and if the French were to enter the town tomorrow, I much doubt whether we should have any Salamancan auxiliaries to assist in cutting our way through them.

That there lately was an ardent spirit of resistance throughout the provinces of Spain has been proved by its effects; and that it has now subsided, we cannot any otherwise account than by supposing that the present directors were inimical to its ardour. No permanent advantage was taken of the first successes against the common enemy; no favourable positions were taken up in a country formed by nature for self-defence; no decisive measures were adopted to preserve the awakened flame of patriotism pure and burning. In some parts of the country it was left to languish unnoticed; in others it was damped by the jealousies of the leading men; and at last, where it has appeared in the field, it is likely to be extinguished by the overpowering energy of the French.

They act while the Spaniards deliberate, and the nation will be lost before the supreme council has settled whether its armies are to march to the right or to the left! Indeed I am certain, from what I see of the people, and hear of their directors, that nothing honourable to the country will be done while a central *junta* exists. There appears to be as many interests in that large body as there are members:—hence, no chief military command is likely to be appointed. All are on the gape in expectation of its acts; and expecting that everything is to be effected by the wisdom of the *junta*, individuals forget the vigour that lies in every single arm; they forget that in these cases the voice of the people is the voice of God; that an armed nation rushing at once upon their oppressors, carry with them the sword of Omnipotence,

The provincial *juntas*, following the example of the central, attend to their own petty emulations, instead of sacrificing all to the generous ambition of freeing their country; while they wait to gain particular points, the end of their meeting is forgotten; the patriotic ardour of the lower classes is wasted in vain declamation; no troops are organized; and the field is left open for the enemy whenever he chooses to come; and, like Cromwell; with one stroke of his mace break up their ruinous *cabals*.

Owing to these *junta* dissensions no plan has been formed by which the country might derive any good from our arrival. Nothing has been arranged relative to our future military operations; and I know that at this moment our commander in chief at Salamanca cannot obtain any, regular communication with the generals of the patriotic forces. Judge then, for you know the delicate honour of his mind, what must be the present state of his feelings, to be shut up in this city at the head of a fine army rendered, at such a crisis useless; but whose powers, if properly aided by the people we came to assist, would soon make Spain the triumphant breach on which rescued Europe would mount to freedom and to glory.

Should the defeat of Castanos prove an authentic report (alas! that we should be listening to reports rather than furnishing some brave subject for them), we shall then have no army with which to act in concert. And if the people be not roused by such misfortunes to take up arms themselves, the whole weight of the campaign will fall upon us. The event you can guess; for although Sir John Moore will exert his talents and military powers to the utmost to fulfil his duty to his country; and to accomplish the object of his command; yet ultimate success must depend on the energy with which the Spaniards will support our efforts. Thirty thousand men, which comprise the whole of our force, cannot for any length of time, nay perhaps not in the contest of one battle, oppose, without instant annihilation, the accumulating hosts of France.

Therefore, if the immense army of Castanos be indeed beaten, into what a strait have we been led by the thoughtless, indeed criminally careless information of the Spaniards! Brought into plains with nothing but our infantry; and our auxiliaries leaving the way open for the enemy, our hands have been tied, and ourselves made a sort of prisoners, even by the people we came to defend. Should we be fortunate enough to be rejoined by General Hope with the cavalry and artillery, we shall certainly be better appointed to resist an attack; but to make any impression by our own movements is now rendered almost impossible. Without a considerable change in the vaunted Spanish patriots now sleeping on their arms, even our junction, with hope, I fear, will not empower us to advance. Hence, in my opinion, the next alteration we make will be towards the mountains of Portugal.

From the brave honesty of Sir John Moore, I have no doubt of his informing ministers at home of the true state of Spain; and of how shamefully the *junta* has misled them, by its representations of the patriotic zeal and military preparation of the nation, That the Spaniards did not continue as the *junta* found them was its own fault. Oppressed and outraged by the French, with a wild revenge hordes of enraged people rose in every quarter of the kingdom: their sudden and impetuous vengeance carried all before them; the veteran armies of France were destroyed, the usurper driven from his assumed capital, and the cry of restitution resounded everywhere. This was the sympathetic act of a whole nation; and this was the fortunate moment for a virtuous nobility to have turned it to their country's advantage. Had some great spirit seized this conquering body, and guided it with the singleness of aim which actuated the soul of Pelagio, when, at the head of his zealous Asturians he drove the invading Saracens over his native mountains, we should not now be shut up in Salamanca, nor would the flying Spaniards be seeking a temporary refuge in their dishonoured homes.

These unhappily constituted *juntas* have, been the origin of a sad failure where the brightest consequences might have been expected. The jealousies of the provincial councils, and the narrow-sighted policy (if not something worse) in the supreme, have changed action into sound; and instead of deeds worthy of record, we see nothing but manifestos; and have the mere words of honour, victory, and glory, presented to us instead of the substance. The first patriots of the revolution were still under arms with Blake, Castanos, and Palafox: but unsupported with new levies, and their leaders trammelled by the distracting orders of the *junta*, the armies gradually mouldered away under the pressures of want and of the returning enemy. And, if the report be true that they are now beaten to their last legion, we are left alone in the midst of a desolated and conquered country, to maintain, unfurled, the already blighted standard of Spanish liberty!

There is something more than unfortunate in this, certainly, consummate folly; and we might be led to suspect a little treachery also. However, I will be sufficiently candid with the *junta* to believe that they are guiltless of any intention to mislead us; but occupied in private battles for individual power, they neglect the public interest: and sacrificing Spain to their intrigues, it is not to be wondered at that her allies should share in the disaster.

I was interrupted at the close of the last sentence by the entrance of a brother officer. The fatal news is too true; the central army is destroyed, and Castanos has fled to Cuenca: and whether the blame rest in or out of the *junta*, I will not pretend decisively to judge, but it is the general opinion that some pretended patriots of rank have played the traitor, and immolated this brave army to the gold of Bonaparte. Wretches so disgraceful to mankind are unworthy to live: and when discovered, I hope the indignation of a betrayed people will devote them to such exemplary punishment, that all who might be inclined hereafter to adopt their baseness may be terror-struck and warned by their fate.

Napoleon is not more a conqueror by arms than by bribery; and while there are base spirits amongst the rulers of a country, neither its liberty nor its existence is safe. A treason of this kind having once been shewn is fraught with evil; it renders the people mistrustful of their counsellors, soldiers fear to follow generals to the field who may have already sold them to the enemy; and a great nation shrinks from trusting its troops in aid of another the rulers of which can be tempted to betray their most sacred interests. In short, suspicion once excited is not easily allayed: it is the very torch of discord; and, I fear, will burn up every patriot exertion in Spain.

A very short time must shew how the defeat of Castanos will affect our movements. Indeed our circumstances will not allow of much deliberation; and the only thing that can make us hesitate about immediate removal is the situation of General Hope. When he forms his expected junction with our commander in chief, you may then anticipate the intelligence that we have fallen back upon the Portuguese frontiers. Meanwhile, as I am unwilling that you should leave Salamanca without seeing all that is worthy notice, I shall proceed to give you a little sketch of this celebrated city.

You will say that instead of a soldier's camp, with all the pomp, pride, and glorious circumstance of war, or a traveller's gay excursions among villas and polite society, I do nothing but play the pilgrim, and lead you about from one holy fabric to another. But have patience with me! as I am not one of those poetical narrators who can amuse with descriptions of what is not in sight, you must even be content with sombre reality, and follow me quietly through the churches of this university. Besides, who knows but this consecrated walk may be only a short preparation of my steps to take a larger one through that holy place of infinite magnitude, where the names of sects are lost; no superstitious absurdity is admitted, and all is peace, truth, charity, and happiness! With this in prospect, you will not now object to enter with me into the church of St. Dominique!

This building, which is attached to the monastery of the Carthusians, is a fine specimen of the same stile of Gothic exhibited in the cathedral; being simple within, but a grotesque assemblage of saints, vegetables, and monsters without. However, I prefer it before the metropolitan church; for there is one addition which greatly improves the effect of the whole; a low and flat arch is thrown over the centre aisle, overshadowing the place beneath, and giving a solemn and mysterious air to that quarter, admirably adapted to the catholic ceremonies. The white habits of the fathers seen in this dim light, and the black veiled Spanish females on their knees, who rest immoveable, and like clusters of ebon pyramids, while mass is said, animate the vaulted temple with appropriate and picturesque groups.

The walls are hung with large pictures wretchedly executed; and a gorgeous piece of gilded carved work decorates the eastern end. A few paces in front of the great altar a figure of the Virgin Mary sits enthroned She is arrayed as I have before described, and bears in her arms the infant Saviour. The sacred pair are placed upon a sort of *brancard*, which has four handles issuing from the corners, for the convenience of carrying it in processions. Amongst the paintings on the left range of Gothic columns are half a dozen daubed effigies of the ancient fathers of this institution, represented in the act of walking forth, carrying their heads in their hands. The stroke of severation must have been done very neatly, for not one drop of blood appears to have been shed on their pale garments.

Wonderful as this emblazonment may seem, the Carthusian saints do not appear to have got a patent for such extraordinary perambulation; for, I remember that one of our Saxon monarchs lost the contact between his head and his neck either by malice or mistake; and being extremely vexed at so unexpected a privation, he took up the ravished member and marched out, bearing it aloft in his hand, and calling on his people to avenge the insult. Ireland too can boast a similar miracle. Her tutelar saint converted this valuable part of his person into a very useful machine. Being pressed at Holyhead for a conveyance to carry him to his favourite land, he took his head from his shoulders, and placing it between his legs, rode on it across the waves which divide the sister isles.

This active journey was to enable the sacred hero to come up with and to kill an evil-minded personage, who had previously set sail in a bark deeply laden with serpents and poisonous reptiles of all sorts, intending to land them on the hitherto pure shores of Ireland. But the speed and virtue of St. Patrick's head got the whip hand of the malignant adventurer; and his immediate death, as well as the destruction of his cargo, prevented any one in future from undertaking a similar enterprise. I need not add, that the place whence the good man commenced his voyage has ever since, in commemoration of the event, been called Holy Head.

Being now in the venerable cloisters of St. Dominique, I cannot leave them without recounting an adventure which, under their hallowed roof, befell our mutual friend Captain ——. Hearing that a grand *Te Deum* was to be performed there, to invoke a blessing on the united arms of Spain and England, curiosity led him to be one of the audience. He found the holy place billed with the laity of Salamanca, besides the white brotherhood and flocks of *religieuse* of every rank from the neighbouring monasteries. The consecrated part of the congregation were arranged on either side of the main body of the church, clothed in all their sacerdotal attributes, and holding the sacred implements of their function. A very large standard, fringed and tasselled, and on which was painted or worked the figure of the saint, was held in the hands of a priest of the highest order. This hallowed production is never brought forth but upon the most extraordinary occasions.

Our friend, unconscious of being himself an object of any attention, was standing very composedly listening to the loud swell of the organ, and the still louder voices of the tonsured choir, when a monk approached him respectfully, and saying something relative to a standard, took his hat from him, and at the same time taking his hand. Captain ——, who did not clearly understand what was said, supposed he was going to conduct him to a spot more convenient for seeing the religious ceremonies; judge, then, his surprise on finding himself not only led up to the consecrated banner of St. Dominique, but at having it placed in his grasp!

At that moment the monks left him to be the supporter of their holy ensign; and a cloud of incense issuing from the surrounding censers, covered the flag and its holder. Imagine the feelings of our friend! to be thus made a partaker in papiastical rite; and placed in a situation so conspicuous, and so hazardous of offending those we came to befriend, should he to resist this enforced honour: however, the sudden roar of the organ, and the pealing voices of the fraternity, with the rapid advance of the marshalled *corpsdes religieuse*, interrupted his amazed cogitations; and hurried him forward like a stream, still bearing in proud array the sainted standard; Though reluctant to make one in such an exhibition, yet as he had been seized upon, and presented with the flag as a testimony of the Spanish church's amity with that of England; he would not, in common charity and prudence, but behave with all requisite decorum and respect.

I believe it was the first time that so revered an appendage of the Roman Catholic faith was entrusted to the hand of a heretic. With a grave countenance he obeyed his fate; and the procession moved on, amidst a renewed burst of sacred minstrelsy. They passed through the great entrance—made rather a long circuit of the city; entering several cloisters and consecrated places; and halting at certain spots, where the holy singing again burst forth; and our friend was occasionally enveloped from the eyes of the attendant multitude by the vast volumes of smoking frankincense which rolled around him.

After his patience and his arms were heartily fatigued by his ponderous load, the party retraced their steps, and re-entered the church of St. Dominique: on gaining the original place whence the, standard had started, a long prayer was said, another cloud of fragrance filled the air, and Captain —— resigned his sacred trust into the hands of the superior priests. His hat was given to him, and he gladly retired down the line of monks, being bowed and sung out of the church till he reached the open air. When fairly escaped from sight, he literally took to his heels, congratulating himself that an exhibition so inimical to the simplicity of his own faith had terminated without any restiveness on his side, and consequent affront on the part of our devout allies. He told me that he had the honour to precede the holy Virgin in this march, and that she brought up his rear, clad in all the costly apparel of the loom and the jeweller's shop,

When I asked him how he could bring his, conscience to be a partaker in this mummery, his reply was,—"I certainly would not have volunteered it: but in carrying a flag though a few streets, I neither worshipped stocks nor stones, nor subscribed to any repugnant doctrine. For peace sake I accepted a civility paid to my country; and by my compliance, I hope I have shewn the people that we are as willing to be tolerant of their prejudices, as they have declared themselves to be of our faith."

Our friend's answer was very commendable; and, orthodox as you are, I believe you will agree in that opinion with your ever sincere &c.

LETTER 14

Salamanca, Dec. 1808.

My Dear S ——,

Having penetrated with you into the cloisters of the religiously immured of our own sex, you will not refuse to accompany me to the mysterious dwellings of the fair vestals of this priest-hallowed city! I will not draw so unmercifully on your regrets as to take you through all the prisons of fading beauty I have lately visited; but it being the one where perhaps the fewest youthful victims are now secluded, I will lead you to the nunnery of St. Clara,

I went thither yesterday with a party of our officers, but could not obtain admittance beyond the outer hall: however, the sisterhood deigned to open the greats door which led out of the convent into this apartment, and which would otherwise have divided us from them; and presenting us with chairs we seated ourselves in a semi-circle before its threshold, and held a discourse much more conveniently than if we had been reduced to the Thisbe-like expedient of conversing through the chinks of the door.

Most of these ladies were rather ancient; yet many wore the remains of past beauty, and filled one with sad reflections that such charms should have been doomed to bloom and fade, and die unseen, unappreciated, unbeloved. But these regrets were to ourselves, our gentle companions did not seem to partake them: they were even, gay, and prosecuted the conversation with a vivacity which shewed they were pleased with our visit; nay, they even paid us compliments which few of the sex who had not forsworn their interest in such qualifications would have ventured to pronounce. They spoke highly of our nation, extolled its military men for the respect we had shewn to them; and said, how very handsome Englishmen were, how captivating their manners! Of course we could not do less than bow to these frank expressions of approbation, and replying to them in kind; they next descanted on the probable approach of the French to Salamanca, and declared their wish to be enabled to fly to England before the completion of such a calamity.

Their dress was of coarse grey woollen cloth; a wrought linen hood bound their heads and necks: each nun wore her rosary; and an exquisite cleanliness gave the finishing charm to their saintly persons. Thirty sisters, I understood, was then the number of the establishment. This order is the strictest of any in the church, and it boasts many canonised heroines; it owes its institution to a female named Clara, how long ago I am not antiquarian enough to tell you; but weary of the pomps and vanities of this wicked world, she fled from them, and secluding herself in the church of St, Damian in the holy city of Asis, there passed a right, pure, and sober existence; doing acts of such charitable import as unquestionably rendered her worthy of the honours she received after her death. Some other virgins becoming enamoured of her peaceful retirement, followed her into the cloister; and so from her and them arose the order of St. Clara.

As a double consecration of the vestal institution, Dona Urraca, an aged maiden of devout practices and chaste thoughts, left the haunts of men, and taking up her abode in an hermitage called Santa Maria, within the trails of this city: on its very site how stands the convent of St. Clara. From its foundation to the present times, the fame and strictness of its unsullied inhabitants, as well as the rare discipline set forth in the Claraen rules, gave a consequence to the sisterhood which claimed the approbation of their sovereign and the pope, and almost idolatrous veneration from the people.

His holiness of Rome granted them many bulls, dispensations, protections, and donations of precious relics; and even so early as in the year 1244, kingly bequests, and rich presents from repentant nobles, poured into the treasury of St. Clara. From this root sprung many a scion; and in every province of this populous countrymen were planted convents of every order, in devout emulation of these happy sisters of Salamanca. So much for vestals in will as well as in deed! I must now give you a hint of some who are so only in name; I mean the fair inhabitants of a few nunneries which lie on the Portuguese frontiers: they did not even keep a threshold between our curiosity and their seclusion.

We found as free ingress into their cells as if we had been a regiment of confessors; their veils were thrown aside, their holy abstinence neglected, and adventures truly romantic ensued. I fancy more than the history of Rousseau's nun was here realised in a hundred instances; and could these lovely forsworns have seen any prospect of safety by flight, I believe many of our officers would have had a daughter of the church added, to his baggage. However, not intending to betray their secrets, and having seen them left to their tears, I shall drop the subject, and turn from what might be sad to graver matters; namely, the students of Salamanca.

The university of this once famous city was founded by Alphonso the Ninth sometime about the year 1222, and established on a similar plan with that instituted at Plasentia by Don Alphonso King of Castile, surnamed the Good. The privileges of the schools in Salamanca were greatly increased by Alphonso the Tenth; a prince whose taste for literature is yet the object of reverence in Spain; and, though unfortunate in his projects, the beauty of his own literary works, and the usefulness of the history he caused to be compiled, well entitle him to his appellation of "The Wise."

The ancient consequence of this place, like the ruins of Palmyra, is daily mouldering away. In the era of its splendour the students were calculated at more than 30,000, and now it scarcely boasts 4,000; indeed, from what I see I should think it difficult to muster half that number. One reason for the present desertion of the university is highly honourable to the students: on the first burst of patriotic enthusiasm in the country, several hundreds of them turned out; and those who were not slain in the late melancholy defeats are yet in arms. From different causes the convents, monasteries, and other public institutions have greatly diminished of their inmates; and the once populous seat of learning and repository of holy men has become a mass of useless edifices falling to decay, and which would be left for the *fox to look out at the window*, were they not now occupied by our troops.

The most attractive feature in the city is the Great Square, which is indeed beautiful. Its *piazza*-walks are the daily lounge of our officers, the students of the colleges, and whatever personages are allured thither by the hope of news. During one of my strolls I entered the cloisters of the monks of St Augustine, and found their walls covered with very frightful paintings of the members of the fraternity who had suffered martyrdom. Various, and exceedingly horrid, were the representations; in many cases they were too shocking to look upon, both on account of the demoniac apparatus of cruelty they portrayed; and because the artist had made, such vile daubing of the whole, that the spectator felt more inclined to laugh at the performance than to reverence the poor tortured saint. In one of these delectable designs a holy man is seen on his knees in a dark and dreary dungeon, an angel is entering at the upper comer, whilst a set of hideous people are looking in and grinning through the bars of the prison.

Behind the praying figure is a large cat in a very attentive posture. After much wondering at the reason of such an introduction, and poring into the picture, I at last discovered the cause of it in a dark part of the canvas, gnawing something like a pair of breeches which, lay on the matted bed of our sacrificed hero. This culprit was a hue rat; and I presume the cat was in the act of meditating revenge for the sacrilegious deed.

As I understood that there is an allegory in this picture, representing the immediately threatened fate of the poor saint, I must of necessity seek it in this part of the design, consequently the breeches of the holy man are intended as emblems of himself, the rat devouring them personifies the blood-thirsty people at the door, waiting to see him brought out to martyrdom; and the cat must allegorise no less a personage than the angel, who is on the watch to rescue the saint, as she is the breeches, from the fangs of the enemy.

From this specimen you may form an idea of what were the other miserable pictures which emblazoned these hallowed walls. A little onward I saw the shrine of their founder, whose miracle-working relics had attracted a no inconsiderable number of waxen infants, legs, arms, thumbs, noses, &c. Not having need of the Æsculapian saints to perform any marvels on my person. I shall make my bow to their altar, and take a circuit through the square to learn what is likely. to be our measures now that the central army of the patriots is lost.

That a retreat is preparing I have no doubt; several quarter-master-generals have been sent to the rear of our present position: and the sick and stores are ordered to Almada. Last night a courier was dispatched to Sir David Baird; I do not certainly know for what purpose, but I should suppose to advise his falling back either on Vigo or Corunna, or to retreat into Portugal. Sad mortifying words, these, my good friend! and that I may not repeat them in this sheet, I hasten to subscribe myself yours.

LETTER 15

Salamanca, Dec. 1808.

My Dear S——,

After the advantages gained by the French troops over the army of Castanos and Palafox, the latter retired to Zaragossa, and the victors advanced to Madrid. They attacked the place, but received some checks; as the inhabitants, aware, of their danger, had with expedition fortified the most vulnerably points. This resolution is certainly in the spirit we expected to have found pervading the whole country; but as it is without able direction, and hopeless of support, I fear their efforts will prove abortive; and that the loss of the capital must speedily follow the defeat of their generals.

Should Spain fall under the yoke of France! it will not have been to the supineness of the people that she owes her slavery; but to the rulers, to whose guidance those very people entrusted themselves, and on whose wisdom they relied. Unhappy nation! as a free man and as an ally, I mourn your approaching fate; and while I respect the gallant peasantry of your mountains as men worthy of their cause, I execrate from my soul the wretches in power who barter your liberties and their own. for victory in a debate; a little temporary influence; or, finally, for the gold of their enemies!

Thanks to a rare instance of bad information in our adversary; General Hope with, his troops and the artillery have arrived unmolested. From this circumstance I do not, doubt that the French, are persuaded we are, already far on our retreat to Portugal; but in this they are deceived; and. what is more, they have failed in forcing us to the measure. Something sudden, we know not what, has, altered the appearance of our dispositions. Instead of moving as we expected, when I closed my last letter, many detachments of our army have marched hence, taking the direct road towards Valladolid. Head-quarters, follow the day after tomorrow; a sight which will be very delightful to this city. The inhabitants, ignorant of the causes of our sojourn, having lately evinced suspicion and discontent at the length of time we have garrisoned their walls.

It would be an ungrateful task now to tell them, that the ill-advised route we had received from their government, as well as the indecision of the *junta* relative to their own proceedings, and the ignorance we had been kept in with regard to the plans of the Spanish military, with which we expected to co-operate; had not only rendered our arrival in the country useless, but even made it appear as if they intended to betray us into the hands of the enemy. To remonstrate with these rulers would now be a vain attempt: the time for successful action has been allowed to pass; and owing to their want of unity, our indefatigable zeal in coming hither is made of no effect; and they have blasted, perhaps forever, the dawning liberties of their country. By dividing their forces; by giving disjointed commands; the whole has been successively annihilated. Advantages have been neglected, and as little attention paid to the maintaining favourable positions, and the organization of recruits, as if the land lay in the profoundest security. The dreadful catastrophe of the patriotic hosts must have undoubtedly increased our difficulties; but as a regular communication has at last been instituted between Sir John Moore and the Spanish government, we may hope that future disasters may be avoided. Indeed, if it were possible to be sanguine in the midst of such destruction, we might be led, by the aspect of the present moment, to augur some good.

We are not to retreat, but to advance!—An order we should gladly have obeyed weeks ago; but better late than never: and as so great a change from the obvious movement has taken place, the general sentiment is, that some advantage, not dreamt of by those out of the secret, is foreseen by the dictators of this onward march. Great indeed must it be to warrant the proceeding of so inferior an army as ours to meet the victorious and accumulating legions of the French.

Such is the conversation with us: but, in my own private opinion, I cannot perceive whence any advantage is now to arise, I know there are none to spring from Spain, as it now lies beaten and humiliated: and to expect that the enemy will give us any, is a fancy more wild than Don Quixote's encounter with the windmills. He never hesitates nor lingers; his blow precedes even his threat; and, like our own Peterborough of the last age—

So wonderful's his expedition,
He's with you like an apparition!

I, therefore, bask not my military ardour in such extravagant imaginations; but in sober probability suppose that our brave commander in chief has received urgent wishes from home that he would not retreat. The descendants of the conquerors at Cressy and Poictiers are not so liberal to their Parthian generals as the Greeks were to the retreat of the ten thousand; nor as the Romans were, when the senate sent to thank the defeated consuls for not despairing of Rome.

Perhaps the promulgators of these, orders for our advance deemed it a measure of kindness to the Spaniards; as, by diverting the attention of the foe, it may permit the discomfited armies to rally; and while he is watching us in the north, leave Madrid a chance of standing her ground, and the south free to collect her patriot strength, and again pour it upon her invaders.

If Sir John Moore have not received these hints from your side of the ocean, I can only attribute our advance to that spirit of enters prise which is so essential in a general who commands in this rapid mode of warfare. He may have received intelligence, not yet breathed to us, that the main body of the enemy which we expected to be now in front of us, has either remained at Burgos, or has weakened itself by sending detachments towards the capital: also having General Hope, with our long wished-for artillery, &c. closing upon us; and finding that our junction with Sir David Baird is secure, (—his cavalry being at Torro,—) our commander may consider, that thus concentrated, we shall not only be strong in ourselves, but may place some reliance on the new and ascertained communication with the *junta*; and by its influence, may expect that the Gallicians and Asturians will not only be called upon, but be properly appointed to join the Marquis de la Romana, and to support us.

Whatever be the grounds of these hopes, may heaven grant us success! I have no alarm for ourselves. Should the provinces meet us with the enthusiasm promised; and their rulers make a proper use of their zeal; all may yet be retrieved. But at the worst, should every Spaniard desert us, we are yet a *phalanx* of British soldiers! The sea is before us; and we have swords to cut a passage to our own element.

Every preparation is made for our march. I hope in the course of a few days to be within sight of those we have journeyed so far to fight; and if we come in contact, shall we not *embrace them with a Briton's arm?*—Alas! that so many disadvantages, which we could neither foresee, nor, situated as we have been, pro-vide against; that they should meet us in a friendly country! A vast and victorious army menacing our few thousands: we, unsupported, and without prospect of resource, should we be defeated! Our enemy, if thinned of half his ranks, has myriads thronging on behind to make up the deficiency. We are liter-ally a forlorn hope; and all we can do is to assert the honour of England, and to sell our lives dearly.

Though ignorant of the state of this province when we came into it, we are tolerably aware of the devastation we are to meet on our departure. The country we must march through has already been drained by the troops recently quartered there. But we cannot doubt that this evil is provided against, and (if practicable) measures must have been taken to convey victual-ling for the army from Corunna, or whatever *depôts* we have formed on the coast. That such has been the precaution of our leaders is my hope; for I can assure you I have no expecta-tions on that head either from the produce of the provinces themselves, or from any inclination in the natives to part with a portion of their scanty subsistence. A voluntary assistance being thus unpromising, we place still less dependence on the aid of magistrates to enforce by their authority, the justice and necessity of the people's yielding us a share of their provision.

These civil officers are everywhere as feeble in their efforts to accommodate us, as they are strong in opposition to their respective *juntas*: and that any orders have arrived from the supreme council to command that we shall be duly supplied is, I hardly think, probable; for, judging of the present by the past, these "grave and reverend *seignors*" seem never awake to what ought to be done till they have overslept the opportunity.

Our enemies teach a more summary mode of acquiring all requisites for subsistence, whether on a friendly or a hostile march: but honour prevents our using force where we do not meet inclination. I hope this delicacy may continue; for when compulsion once begins, the compellers often over-step their orders, and ravage where only a little indispensable foraging was intended.

Preparations are now made for head-quarters to be put in motion; and when we march out, which Sir John Moore proposes to do on the 13th of this month, we shall have just past one month in this city, having entered it on the 13th of November! a stay that we all lament as lost time; and, calculating the weeks irretrievably wasted here, with the many we lingered out in Portugal after the convention of Cintra, we cannot but exclaim in bitterness of soul, "Had the decision for our advance been earlier made, the first snows of winter would have found us at the feet of the Pyrenees; and probably the rear of our army would have possessed itself of Vittoria on the 4th of November, instead of that of Bonaparte!"

Promptitude, determination, and rapidity, have raised the chief of the French nation to the height where he now stands; and the contrary proceeding (as all who mark the history of Europe for these few late years must be convinced) has levelled the states of the continent to where they now lie, even at his footstool

I shall write again from our next halt, hoping that it may be to better purpose than the last: I, meanwhile, bid you *adieu*!

Sahagun, December, 1808.

My dear S——,

We left Salamanca at eight o'clock on the morning of the 13th; having assembled at the Zamora gate, where the baggage belonging to head quarters was collected and placed under a guard of infantry and cavalry. At the appointed moment all moved forward, forming one of the most active and interesting scenes I ever beheld. The morning was fine, beautifully illuminating the surrounding landscape, and imparting a delightful glow to the busy exhilaration of our spirits. All the sombre prognostications on the late disasters which had clouded our hopes while in quarters, vanished from our minds like the fading recollections of a frightful dream.

Every object was calculated to inspire confidence. The passing wagons groaning under the weight of ammunition, the trains of artillery, and the well-appointed columns, accompanied by hundreds of mules; the continued hum of the mingled voices of thousands seemed to people the air; and the more distant part of the country filled with myriads of living creatures moving over the far-stretching plain; the soldiers' bayonets glittering in the rising rays of the sun; the proud prance of cavalry; batmen and servants leading spare horses; and groups of women and children mounted on asses; with hordes of followers of all descriptions, driving heavy laden mules hung with bags, trunks, and portmanteaus; formed, altogether, a scene of animation, and of military array that enchanted the soul, and seemed to promise a happy rencontre with our enemies.

We found the road excellent; but owing to the multitude of our host, and their consequent encumbrances, our march was not of the quickest, which rather annoyed the eager spirits of those who wished to press on. The country was flat for a considerable extent of way; but became a little hilly as we approached Carnizal, the village destined to receive us for the night; it was at the distance of six leagues from Salamanca.

Carnizal being a place of small dimensions, Sir John Moore proceeded, without halting, to the town that was to be our next day's rest. Many of our troops, also, took up their quarters there,

When we recommenced our march we found the road still good, but flat as before. It afforded us a view of at least thirty spires of churches arising from the bosom of distant villages. Aliajos, where we rejoined our commander in chief, stands amidst these numerous rustic settlements; and is a town of some consequence; possessing a handsome square, with two churches of considerable magnitude.

A beautiful castle, which commands the entrance of the place on the Salamanca side, is the most lofty object seen from the plain, and gives to the neighbouring buildings that air of power and dignity which is peculiar to fortress towns. From the architecture of this noble structure, which is in a style of modern regularity never observed in the works of the earliest ages, I am led to think that it is not very ancient. Its form is square, and flanked with four round towers; one of which is larger than the others, and very high. Its outer wall is guarded by regular bastions; and a well excavated ditch cuts off any egress from without.

This last part of the work is of an immense depth, and is crossed on the north side by a drawbridge, the stone supports of which still remain. At some distance from the town stands a monastery of begging friars. How opposite are the meditations which these two different orders of buildings suggest! The one entirely tranquil, the other all tumult. The former state is not envied by us at present: we are but just launched into the turbulent waves; and as we have already successfully breasted a few of them, you will excuse us if we do not think of rest, till having surmounted them all, we jump victorious on the British shore.

A party of our dragoons under the command of General Stewart, yesterday fell in with some of the enemy's cavalry, and after a brisk contest soon made them prisoners. This is the first affair between us and the forces of Napoleon since we left Portugal; we find the French officers very pleasant men, and far from chagrined by their misfortunes. Indeed, I believe they inwardly rejoice at having fallen into our hands, rather than into those of the Spaniards, as they well know the enraged patriots would have given them no quarter; nay, to put the idea beyond a doubt, mobs of our allies have continually surrounded the house in which our prisoners were confined, awaiting the moment when they hoped we would call the Frenchmen out and have them shot. But that way of disposing of our fellow creatures who have confided themselves to our honour not being in our laws of war, we disappointed our sanguinary friends; and contrived to preserve, without farther molestation, the lives of our captive enemies.

The following morning we renewed our march under a thick fog which enveloped us almost the whole way to Torro; a circumstance I much regretted, having been informed by several of our officers who had previously visited that city that the views between it and Aliajos were exquisitely interesting. The road being on the banks of the river Duero was sufficient to excite the most romantic anticipations in my mind; but the envious mist hid them all from my eyes, and allowed me nothing but the unsatisfactory shadows of imagination, where I expected to meet the beautiful realities of nature.

The city we are drawing towards is not inferior in size to Salamanca. It stands on the ridge of a high hill, overlooks the Duero, and commands the whole plain beneath. The approach to it from below is extremely striking: its mud walls, lofty spires, and ancient castle, stretch along the brow of a dark brown mountain, A fine bridge of many arches crosses the river: the centre arch has been destroyed, but is now restored, though in no very lasting a manner.

A party of our Gallic friends having been in the town not many days before our arrival, left orders for rations to be provided for the advance of 15,000 men. But so little attention was paid by the magistrates to this formidable intimation, that when we entered, instead of finding preparations of welcome for our enemies, we found "a plentiful scarcity of everything."

We halted a day at Torro, which gave me an opportunity of viewing the buildings, and becoming acquainted with their romantic environs. The great, religious edifice of the city is of an architecture so resembling our Saxon, both in the style of arch and ornament, that I could have imagined the Temple church in London and this on the banks of the Duero to have been designed by the same artist. The principal entrance is by a door profusely decorated with effigies of angels and saints playing on various musical instruments; numbers of which, intermixed with flowers and lace-like fretwork, form the *frieze*.

On the right of the door is an immense mass of granite rudely sculptured into the semblance of the trunk and neck of an animal; I think it is meant for a bull; not because of the likeness do I pay it this compliment, but in consequence of having seen the figure of the same beast represented in different places of the city, and particularly emblazoned on shields attached to the entrances and other conspicuous parts of the city: probably this animal is the armorial bearing of the town; and the name of the place sanctions the supposition. About fourteen more religious houses made up the holy treasury of Torro.

The remains of the ancient mud walls run all round the city. It was a mode of fortification introduced by the Maures (or Moors), to supply the deficiency of stone in this neighbourhood. Earth was also resorted to for even the more elevated works; although I found bricks here of most exquisite manufacture, and fabricated into curious and fanciful ornaments. One fine edifice flanked with richly *friezed* towers and fretted projections, presented a noble specimen of the Moorish architect's abilities. Every step in this town presents some object highly interesting; and nothing can be more picturesque than several points both within and without its walls. It is celebrated for many a warlike rencontre betwixt the Christians and the Infidels; and particularly for a great battle which was fought between Ferdinand of Castile and Alphonso king of Portugal. This memorable victory, obtained by the brave husband of Isabella over his adversaries, took place in the year 1476.

Before I take you farther on our journey I must not omit mentioning, that at Aliajos we found an English messenger, who had brought me letters from England. Recollecting our own owlish forebodings while at Salamanca, I am not surprised at the fear you all express for our safety. Your idea that we had long ago marched from the learned city, and that in consequence of the accumulated defeats of the Spaniards, our danger of being surrounded must be great indeed, was not a very improbable one; but I hope that the return of this courier will satisfy our country that we are not yet in so awful a predicament; not likely to be so ensnared: but if we should, that there is not one British neck amongst us that will consent to pass under the yoke of a French general. We came hither to protect the Spaniards against the enemies of Europe; and sooner than relinquish our post for Gallic chains, we would all earth our heads in Spanish graves.

But this is a gloomy alternative, my friend, which is more in idea than in prospect; our anticipations have nothing to do with the mattock and the spade; so no more evil prognostications from your side of the water, I beg. The papers of a French officer who had been dispatched to Maréchal Soult were taken in consequence of his death, and brought to head-quarters. They will be of use to us, as rumour says that the same military duke is not far off. I wish it may prove true; for, we have now closed nearer on Sir David Baird, who is on the same movement with ourselves; and, I trust, a favourable result of our joint forces will soon be reported by Sir John Moore, as some compensation to our drooping fame, for being so long mewed up within the withering; precincts of Salamanca.

On the 16th we recommenced our march, and took the road towards Castro-Nueva; distant from our last quarters about five leagues. The country gradually assumed an undulating line, and then rose into hills, which were plentifully peopled, if we may judge by the number of villages which decked their sides. Why it should be so well colonized I cannot explain; for the district seemed particularly dreary. Not a tree, nor even a shrub was seen to enrich the barren prospect. Nay, the valleys themselves which intersected these miserable crags boasted not one sprig of verdure higher than a blade of grass, to wave its solitary head over the cheerless waste. This was an apt scene in which to change our climate: it appeared as if by some invisible agency, we had been transported from the luxuriant temperate zone to the naked tracts and chilling blasts of Siberia. The weather became piercingly cold; and the saturated air hung a corroding damp upon us that portended even another alteration for the worse.

On the following morning we pursued our way, which was rendered both unpleasant and difficult by a heavy fall of snow. This circumstance checked the rapidity of our march; it encumbered our footsteps, and beating its icy artillery in our faces, so impeded our advance, that the beams of day had long been set before we gained our quarters, which were at Valderes.

The town is a large one; but yet not sufficiently extensive to accommodate with any degree of comfort the numerous army which we poured into it. On the arrival of myself and party we found it filled with cavalry and infantry, with almost the whole of the artillery; and droves of asses laden with women and children, like gangs of gypsies, crowding the streets. In short, every species of bustle and inconvenience that attends a march in a belligerent country menaced us on our entrance into this city.

No pursuit of man produces such various feelings in the human breast as the events of a campaign. Scenes of exultation and regret chequer the path; but the latter, I am sorry to say, are generally most frequent. Indeed it is truly pitiable to see the trains of women burthened with poor helpless infants, either tied on their backs, or stuffed into the panniers of asses, trudging along, exposed to cold and wet, and all the terrible accidents attending their unassisted situation.

Such sights excite a wish that more determined measures were taken by our military government to prevent these accumulations of the feebler sex following the army. If they be at all requisite at these times, let the number be very limited, and the limitation strictly adhered to. But better, in my mind, would it be to exclude every one of them (at least no children should be permitted to accompany the troops), as they only fill the men with anxieties respecting their safeties and accommodation; and in many cases occupy the conveyances intended for the sick and weary; and consume half the provisions which is necessary for the support of the army. These are certainly objects deserving the attention of the military legislature; and, both for propriety and compassion's sake, I hope our rulers will see the wisdom of taking them into consideration.

I need only mention one instance of the distress this indulgence creates. On the day we left Salamanca, I saw a poor creature bearing her infant in her arms, and following her husband, who was attached to one of the regiments then on its march: she had only three days before brought this misery-doomed babe into life; and, pale and faint, she now dragged her enfeebled limbs along, clasping the little sufferer to her breast. To lend her any assistance was totally out of my power; and with a pain at heart which gave rise to the foregoing reflections, I saw her pass on. Whether she has reached thus far, I am ignorant; but I hardly think her strength would hold out even through the first day's march.

At Valderes the conveniences we had hitherto enjoyed might be sought, but could not be found. The number of our troops occasioned not only the men but the officers to be billeted in crowds together; and for want of sufficient stabling, many of our horses were left in the open air. Here, then, I bade *adieu* to the cleanliness and regularity we had hitherto been enabled to obtain. We were now entering seriously into the privations of war; and this privation, I must own, I do find difficult to bear with the indifference becoming a soldier!

Thanks to a good constitution, and to my creed as a military man, I consider nothing a hardship that leaves me an unmolested person; but filth and vermin are more frightful enemies to your friend than hunger and thirst, and all the *etceteras* of comfort-killing war. However, if a man cannot get rid of this delicacy, he must even prepare to run away from Spain; and as the remedy in our case would be more grievous than the disease, I even plucked up courage to become at once a contented *denizen* of these dirt-infested regions; and like a certain heroine throwing away her camphor-bag, dash my particularities to the winds, exclaiming, "Farewell decency! Welcome nastiness, and all the crawling plagues of Egypt!!"

The morning after our arrival into this initiatory pigsty was ushered in by a rapid and severe frost; and when we walked forth we found the streets and roads covered with upset baggage, tumbled-down mules, and prostrate artillery-horses. The change of weather having been so sudden, the shoes of these invaluable animals had not been turned up; and the hardness of the frost making the ground like glass, they slipped about and fell in every direction.

The cold in this season is more piercing here than in England. And when this is acknowledged, I cannot but be surprised at the inefficient means the natives adopt for its exclusion. Few have glazed windows; some have not even shutters, but allow the searching air to blow unimpeded through the casement into the house. The scanty pan of charcoal you were before made acquainted with is the only thing like a fire you ever see or feel; they have no cheering and glowing grates as we have in our country; all is comprised in this little pot of fuel, and with it they strive to give a hint of warmth to their chambers; and when they want a thawing themselves, they stand round it like the priests of Vesta over the sacred fire.

To keep themselves warm, the lower classes sleep in their

clothes; and seldom knowing the comfort of water, they are, consequently, the dirtiest people in Europe. It would be insufferable to read, were I to give you any idea of the soil and inhabitants of these human worlds; suffice it to say, that it is a great delight to them (an amusement relished as highly as a fox-hunt is by honest John Bull) to seek the population of each other's heads, and to take thence its creeping deer. A similar practice I have seen in many a foreign nation; nay, even in a part of our own empire: the fields of "green Erin," for instance, where the sturdy sons of the ancient Milesians still shew their love of the chace by this sort of heady war.

In Spain such sport is esteemed a great luxury; and that the native on whose person it is performed regards it as an act of kindness the following circumstance will prove.

A friend of mine who visited Madrid in more tranquil moments than the present, while in that city went to the presentation of a new play. Love was not omitted in this piece. The scene drew up, and discovered the enamoured pair embracing and kissing each other with no inconsiderable degree of passion. The modesty of the audience was shocked; and such a universal expression of disapprobation was evinced that the acting was stopped. But the night following the same play was again brought forward, and proceeded very quietly unto the critical scene. The curtain rose, and presented the lovers, but differently employed. The lady was journeying through the ravines, between the long looks of her beloved, and taking thence their affrighted little residents.

At this sight peals of applause rung throughout the house; and the remainder of the piece went off with the loudest acclamations. So much for the most delicate testimony of Spanish tenderness! Where, my good friend, are all the ethereal loves of the Don Ferdinands and Dona Seraphinas of our romances, when we behold such spectacles? I am afraid they have ruined my interest in the heart-smitten heroes and heroines of Spain forever. But, as there is no reason why it should have the same effect on our anxieties respecting their military welfare, I shall proceed with the annals of our campaign.

Our next destination was Majorga; three leagues distant from our last quarters. This place is not inferior in size to Valderes; and boasts the remains of former greatness, a ruined castle and antique fortified walls. During our march we passed through several villages, and saw the inhabitants dressed in their winter garbs. Those thus appropriately attired were labourers and shepherds. The Laplanders could not present a more cold-repelling appearance. A rough goat or sheep skin was fitted to their persons; this, with a sort of conical hood or cowl, of which the pictures of Robinson Crusoe will give you an exact portrait, form their whole contour.

At Majorga we stayed for the night; and, early next morning, renewed our march towards Sahagun, at which place we arrived about three o'clock, after halting on the road for some time; owing to the report of a commissary who, riding forward, heard from the peasants that the French were entering the town. He. instantly returned to impart this intelligence to us; but, on investigating further, we found the account false, and that it arose from the entrance of a party of our own, victorious troops instead of the enemy.

The cavalry under Lord Paget's command having been dispatched in front amongst the neighbouring villages, were ordered to march towards the town we were proceeding to occupy, and which, on the night of the 20th of this month, was in the possession of about 500 French horse. Our gallant Viscount, in executing the proposed plan, fell in with the enemy at the moment of their evacuating Sahagun, and an action took place, in which our brave hussars behaved with their usual steadiness and intrepidity. I was informed by one of his Lordship's staff that this affair was more like the regular movements of a field-day than a warlike encounter, which is generally accompanied with a bustle that wears the appearance of confusion. The French, finding it was impossible to escape, formed across the road to receive our charge. Colonel Grant and Captain Jones, of the 16th, were the only officers wounded; and very few men fell on our side. The enemy in this defeat, being our superior in numbers, lost nearly twenty killed, besides wounded, and 200 taken prisoners, before they took to flight. Most of our brave fellows who felt the edge of the French sword were cut in the head; and that owing to the little defence which the present form of their caps allows. This circumstance shews the necessity of changing the prevailing fashion of fantastic head-dresses in the field, for the less ornamental but more useful helmets of our enemies. Whatever be the fate of this expedition, we should at least make it serviceable to us, by learning all that is to be taught by the great masters of arms, who for these twenty years have been educated in a university of blood and victory. The deuce is in it, then, if we cannot take a lesson from them in the art of shielding the most vital parts of our persons,

Their helmets are light, excellently adapted to guard the head, and at the same time very elegant. They have brass chains which come under the chin, protecting the ears and the sides of the face from a horizontal *coup-de-sabre*. The men who wore furred caps at all resembling our own, had them lined within with a hoop of iron; and from the ears devolved two strong bars. Even with this, heavy appurtenance; their weight did not exceed that of the flimsy, but muff-like appendages that encumber the heads of so many of our soldiers. Indeed, this awkward cap of ours, by being constructed partly of pasteboard, soaks up a great quantity of wet during the violent rains of this country, and so becomes unbearably heavy and disagreeable, while it affords no protection to the wearer. At all times they can be cut down to his skull with the greatest ease. Excepting this defect, every other military appointment of our people, both for themselves and their horses, is superior to that of the French. An excellence which cannot but be perceived by them; while the late rencontres must force them to acknowledge our advantage in still more essential respects.

I happened to be billeted with an officer who had been engaged in the affair of the morning of the 21st. During the combat it was his fortune to cut down a French officer of *chasseurs*. Securing the horse and accoutrements of his discomfited enemy, he ordered them to be taken to his own quarters. When my friend and I met, according to the usages of time immemorial, we examined the spoil; and opening the portmanteau of the fallen hero, we found in it no "dagger, *casque*, or buckler," but a silver ewer and a basin of the same costly metal, beaten close together, I suppose to render them more convenient for package.

Along with the handles of a few silver knives and forks were a thousand glittering trifles and trinkets which the plunder of the chapels, perhaps the person of many a Virgin Mary, had afforded. A richly embroidered jacket also came forth, at whose button-hole hung the *croix d'honeur* of the celebrated Legion of Bonaparte.

With such articles, and so obtained, did one of the honourable members of this redoubted body fill his cloak-bag! I confess I should have found so pitiful as well as shameful a robbery hard to believe had I not been present at the proof. The gentleman was not killed: and being picked up by our men, was brought to Sahagun with the rest of the prisoners. On the intimation of his having survived, my friend, of course, returned to him the whole of this precious deposit; although the stolen goods found on the soldiers of the detachment to which he belonged were the next day sold by public auction in the square of one of the convents.

Maréchal Soult is now not many leagues from our front, and occupies Saldana with an army of 16,000 men. We feel the force which draws us forward redoubled as we approach the point of attraction. If he be as ready to advance as we are to meet him, you will soon have a more interesting detail from your sincere friend.

LETTER 17

Sahagun, December, 1808.

The spirit which animates our troops might *create a soul under the ribs of death*; or, what is still more miraculous, inspire courage, into the bosom of cowardice itself. There is something so active, so buoyant, and at the same time so steady in the eagerness with which they prepare to meet the enemy, that I see in every man who passes me the worthy son of our resistless ancestors of Blenheim and Dettengen.

It is determined that Soult, who is now so near us, shall be immediately attacked. The brilliant affair of the 21st has stimulated the infantry with a redoubled ardour to equal their brethren a cheval; and I trust that the sun will soon rise on another day glorious to England. The more glorious to us, you will say, when you find that it has been achieved by our unsupported selves; for at present there is no appearance of any assistance from our Spanish friends; no armed peasantry is even talked of as likely to turn out; and the *juntas* seem, by their obstinate neglect of all their engagements, to be laying the whole defence of the country upon us; or rather, I ought to say, to have brought us from England merely to fight a battle; a sort of tournament between us and the enemy, to which they expect no consequences.

Should we be victorious, and advance, of which I have little doubt, what will be the result to us? Situated as we are, we cannot increase our numbers; and without an active co-operation on the part of the Spaniards, it will be next to an impossibility to maintain our communications with Vigo or Corunna, while the unobstructed armies of France are pouring into the country from every avenue of the Pyrenees. However we are ready to fight. Our leaders know best why we were not brought where we could do it before; and why our present situation is chosen for our first battle.

Bad as appearances may be, I have such a reliance on the prudence as well as courage of Sir John Moore, that I am certain he would not risk the tarnishing his fame, and the honour of his troops, by bringing them into a situation where either were likely to be injured. I am persuaded that the steps we are preparing to take were not determined on by him without his having conceived an idea of their necessity; that it would do still more than rescue the name of his army from the obloquy which the "great vulgar" as well as the "small," from ignorance of the peculiar situations of the objects they arraign, are ever ready to throw upon what does not exactly meet their expectations.

Not that I believe he would needlessly sacrifice a hair of any man's head who is under his command, to gain the proudest admiration which depends on the prejudging judgements of those whose voice may give popularity, but never can bestow fame. He, with every other veteran, must be aware that it is sometimes the duty of a general to risk the odium of being called too severely cautious; nay, of being stigmatised with the appellation of lukewarmness, and a hundred epithets of the same complexion, rather than purchase acclamations at the expense of humanity; and, by a brilliant rashness, hurry his brave followers into an extremity where death is inevitable. The mob may deify such a valiant fool; but true heroism is to have the courage to refuse as well as to give battle.

The actuating reason with our general, I therefore believe to be his hope that the sight of a signal victory won on our part might arouse the dormant spirit of the natives; and that stimulated by our example, they would again fly to their colours, and be, as we expected to find them, a nation in arms. To gain such an end some extraordinary hazard is worth incurring; for it must be evident to everyone who knows the subject, that the ultimate success of the Spanish cause depends more upon their own exertions than on the efforts of any force we can send into their country.

But should tomorrow night close on a setting ray of Britain's glory; should the superiority of our enemy's number, or the fortune of the Napoleon star, overcloud our destiny; should we fail where we hitherto have been used to conquer; then indeed will our situation be critical. A rapid and miserable re-treat must be the consequence. In the same proportion as we might augur future support from the Spaniards in the case of a victory, should we meet a reverse, we must calculate that so dire a circumstance would send them all far enough from contact with the stricken deer; and we shall be left alone to a desolate country, and a surrounding enemy.

This is, the darkest side of events; and one that we do not ex-pect ever to see: but in all actions of life I think it right to calculate foul, as well as fair, and then no disaster can have the double advantage of taking one by surprise. However, I con-sider a defeat of our army at this juncture so very unlikely, that I have no doubt of tomorrow's success rearing the standard of patriotism again in the bosom of Leon; and that as the natives demonstrate their re-animated enthusiasm, our unfavourable opinions of their zeal may vanish like the flashes of our enemy's artillery.

The long wished-for orders were issued this day, and every req-uisite necessary to meet the events of a battle are prepared; the surgeons have arranged their instruments, and all is set in order in the neighbouring convents, to receive those who may feel too deeply the effects of the encounter. The guns have already moved off; we are to march in two columns this evening at eight o'clock; and by daybreak tomorrow we shall be close to the enemy, that being the appointed time of our approach; the hour in which the flower of the British army will either bloom forth with greater brilliancy, or be cut off, perhaps forever.

Tomorrow evening will be the eve of Christmas Day! When that moon rises which will light our happy relatives in England to the gay convivialities of that joyous, season, how many of their sons, brothers, and friends, may then have been just laid in a bloody grave. Each individual amongst us hopes that this melancholy fate may not be destined, for him, but that he is to be one whom Providence hath ordained to gather the laurels, and to wear them proudly on the British shore. I am as sanguine as the best of them: but yet on my old principle of providing for the worst, when I close this epistle I shall seal it up with others of more moment; and, leaving it with a friend, direct him, in case of my too speedily ascending to the *airy hall, of my fathers,* to forward the packet to England.

I have just had a similar consignment, made to me by a brother officer who has provided us with a detachment of dragoons, Thus we depend on each other in this lottery of life! Whoever draw the prizes will, I hope, pay due attention to these last deposits of their less lucky friends, fated perhaps to meet the blanks of death; and by such fidelity administer the only consolation left to the mourning survivors of the slain.

But let me leave this woebegone tone, and bring you to a little acquaintance with the place we now occupy. A noble and extensive monastery, overspreading half the town, contains all its holy fathers, and affords quarters for some of our troops and the French prisoners. A large market place, with a fine fountain in the centre, is the principal object in Sahagun, which, like every other town in Spain, cannot boast of the wide street. Just beyond the eastern entrance is the field which has so recently been the scene of bloodshed.

I took a walk thither, and found the dead bodies of ten or twelve Frenchmen who had been stripped of their uniforms by the peasantry, lying cold and almost covered with snow. I was surprised to discover a female amongst the group; how she became thus situated it is not easy to guess, unless I may suppose that she was some love-impelled damsel, and followed her soldier to the field; or, that being enamoured like many an Amazon of war for its own sake, she became an appendage of the camp: and here, by some accidental shot, was deprived at once of life and her military ardour.

The battle was fought not far from a convent, and a chapel also is near; so that we might have expected that, if not humanity, common religious decency would have prompted the monks to have shrouded from the rending elements the once animated forms of their fellow creatures and brothers in faith. But it is enough that these poor corpses were once Frenchmen, to excuse every Spaniard to himself for leaving them to all the horrors of exposure, all the direful consequences entailed on their souls by the omission of the church's rites! Thus do these holy men consider the effects of their inextinguishable revenge; and forgetting the charity they preach, they gladly consign their enemies to everlasting perdition. What the consecrated brethren of Plasentia taught me to believe of their spirit of vengeance, the fathers of Sahagun have convinced me is true. I confess that more mercy and less vindictiveness would be more congenial with my zeal; and I presume to think would be more likely to propitiate the God whom they and all Christendom profess to serve.

On my return to my quarters, I approached the door of a nunnery, which, chancing to be open, I entered, and found three nuns, not very juvenile to be sure, but nevertheless to a weary pedestrian rather attractive, as they were giving away wine, and, were in conversation with a secular personage of the softer sex. These kind sisters offered me some of the sparkling beverage which even King Solomon says, *makes glad the heart of man.* I accepted their proffer, and listened attentively to an argument which had already begun between the parties; a sort of debate which superstition would denominate between earth and heaven: but reason would say, between nature and folly.

Our single combatant was a Portuguese female, the wife of one of our muleteers, and who had attended her spouse the whole way from Vimeira; her opponents were the fair sisterhood, then dispensing the truth-inspiring juice. I was much struck by the validity and eloquent reasoning of our female muleteer, both in politics, religion, and feeling. She laid before her veiled friends the criminality of their present comparatively useless way of life; their value in society when properly disposed of, the duties they owed to heaven, the world, and to themselves, with equal ability and convincing pathos, She painted in glowing colours the estimations those women hold in the eye of God who fulfil the end of their being, who make a proper use of the talent entrusted to them; and bring forth and educate beings for utility here and happiness hereafter.

To be sure she not a little shocked the cloistered virgins, by

116

counselling them to follow her example, to *go forth and increase and multiply,* and by giving children to their country, verify the sacred words, that *he who has his quiver full of them, need not fear to speak with his enemies in the, gate.* Indeed, she told them that she looked upon herself, a mother of sons, and a helpmate of her husband, and an assistant to the brave English, to be far more acceptable in the sight of heaven than if she were shut up in a holy cell praying all day for success to the Spanish army.

It was all very true what she said; but as she began, soon afterwards to be a little scandalous on the unseen pleasures which the sisters tasted even in spite of their vows, and yet without giving any living equivalent to the public for the breach of its laws; laws which she persevered in saying were impolite, unnatural, and impious; I thought, for the sake of the fair vestals' blushes, it was but gallantry to take my leave; but not before I heard her declare that since she joined the British army, she had seen more charity exercised by the heretics than she had ever met with in any religious assembly that Portugal produced. As I immediately withdrew, I know not how the dispute was settled; but I have no doubt that however the prejudices of the sainted damsels would militate against her, their hearts whispered a warm assent to her arguments.

However, it was well that our spirit at this time breathed something of freedom through the land; for had the reign of the inquisition been frowning over Spain at this moment, my female friend's nails would have been clipped and her joints made a little looser, to punish the freedom of her tongue. With a thousand grateful remembrances to the reformation which excluded Philip the Second and all his families from our land, I remain your sincere, &c.

LETTER 18

Beneventè, December, 1808.

How great is our disappointment! No advance has taken place, though at the hour appointed the whole of our force were under arms. Even our right column had began its march, and all the rest, in high spirits, were impatiently counting the moments until the word should be given for their starting also. An order was issued; but, oh! my friend, to what purpose! We were to go back to our quarters! *and by daybreak next morning be again under arms.* But not to fight; to retreat! a thunderbolt falling at the feet of each man could not have transfixed them more. The effect this sudden and extraordinary alteration of intention had upon the troops is indescribable. A minute before, and every heart beat high with a resistless courage that longed to rush into the battle. Victory seemed to wave them from the hills. Already they heard the shout of their country on the news of this glorious, day; and with the eager-trembling of unloosed hounds; in sight of their prey, they impatiently awaited the order of release which was to send them like bolts of death upon their enemies.

Think then what was our blank, when at this moment of high-wrought enthusiasm, the order was declared that all must return to their quarters! Every countenance was changed; the proud glow on their cheeks was lost in a fearful paleness; the strongly-braced arm sunk listlessly to the side; a few murmurs were heard, and the army of England was no more. Its spirit was fled; and what appeared to me a host of heroes with anticipated success triumphing in each eye, now dispersed from before me as the mere machines of war, men in arms without hope, wish, or energy.

In my life I never witnessed such an instantaneously withering effect upon any body of living creatures. A soldier can easily stimulate himself to seek glory even in the cannon's, mouth; but to withdraw when she courts his embrace, is a species of self-denial he is not fond of practising. The men, if I may be allowed to use a poetical comparison, having heard the order, slowly departed from their late exulting station like a once effulgent cloud from which the sun has withdrawn its beams, rolling down the mountain in dark and heavy gloom.

Under these circumstances, if we felt this reverse of measures hard to be borne, what must have been the struggle in our brave commander's mind before he could consent thus to damp the ardour of his troops; thus to relinquish a victory within his grasp; and to refuse the splendid glory just bursting over his head! And yet with these temptations beckoning to the field, he had the resolution to reject them all; and decided by cool judgement and a warm humanity, determine to resign the battle.

A courier had arrived very late in the day from the Marquis de la

Romana (who was to have advanced to our support with 6000 men), bringing intelligence that a strong column of French was coming from Madrid on Salamanca, and that Marshal Soult had received a very formidable reinforcement. It was the intimation of these events that determined Sir John Moore to abandon his design of an attack. No other advantage than the winning of the battle could be derived from it; as from the enemy's movements on Salamanca, all attempts of the people to rise would be crushed even in the desire.

This temporary prospect of assistance from the Spaniards being no longer to be entertained, we should be thought victorious, without resources; without recruits to replenish the loss which a battle, however successful, must necessarily occasion. The French, on the contrary, would strengthen themselves every hour; and our day of triumph might almost immediately be followed by one of defeat; and then, cut off from the passes and holds of Gallicia (without the possession of which our retreat cannot be tendered secure, nor can we be supplied from the coast in the case of an entire failure of the country); nothing could await us but alternatives no ways agreeable to our high-raised expectations

These reasons, I am told, decided our return. The hard resolution once made, no time was lost in carrying it into execution; and the following morning Generals Hope and Fraser fell back. On Christmas-day we followed; but no longer, my friend; with the gay plumage of war, the exulting hope and herald-voice of victory. Heavy, heavy, we trod along; although our retiring motion was ordered to be as expeditious as possible, that we might seek a more advantageous position in a less unfavourable country.

The sacred season so celebrated at home, with happiness and good cheer was greeted by us with misery and no cheer at all; and what was worse, not the prospect of any to replenish our exhausted spirits through the fatiguing dreariness of a retreating march. Majorga at that time held my person; and sharing my "spare fast" with two or three companions, we pleased ourselves with the sublime hint of Milton, that we were *dieting with the gods*. And when we found the meditation too ethereal an aliment, we tried to nourish ourselves with the ideas of more substantial fare, and fed upon the hopes of catching some sort of dinner next day.

Never had any philosophers more in their power than we poor soldiers were now furnished with, to disprove Hume's famous theory of ideas and realities being of the same substance. Had there been the least truth in such doctrine; while thinking on the roast beef of old England and its huge plum-puddings, we should not have remained an army of starving wretches on Christmas-day, ready to devour one another for very hunger.

On the 26th, we pursued our way, directing our march towards Beneventè; leaving Valderes to our left; passing over a tolerably good road; and crossing the river Esla about two leagues from the city we were approaching, we mounted a line of hills along which we proceeded till its opposite side opened Beneventè to our view. Having descended this row of heights, and again passed over the same river by a strong and noble bridge, we crossed a plain of nearly two miles in extent, and reached the base of the eminence on which the town rears its embattled walls.

The first appearance of this our destined halting-place presented a picturesque effect; and on a nearer investigation, we find it replete with objects of interest. Its principal ornament is the castle, anciently the residence of the Dukes of Beneventè. It is now a superb mansion, and formerly must have been a powerful fortress. The architecture is of a mingled Moorish and Gothic taste, executed in the finest and most elaborate style. Its turrets are rich infretted ornaments, and many of them are bound round their summits with a huge stone chain admirably sculptured. The north front of the castle is almost entirely open; being formed of ranges of Moorish arches supported by columns of porphyry and granite. So much for the outside: the inside is not less magnificent.

The grand saloon, on whose tesselated floor stands a collection of beautiful pillars, is of an immense size; and I counted more than an hundred and fifty of these costly supports Its roof is profusely painted, gilded, and chequered with a thousand colours, and still farther adorned with the most intricate carvings. *Friezes* of porcelain, in a kind of damask pattern, conveying a rude resemblance of what we so much admire in the Etruscan taste, wind round this vast hall. At one end of it is an immense *basso relievo* of St. George killing the dragon, which is also executed in porcelain. Niches, alcoves, and excavated seats in all parts of the walls, and loaded with a variety, and splendour of ornamental most painful to dwell on, raise their arched heads amid labyrinthian twinings of gold, silver, gorgeous colours, and curiously diversified grotesque work, Countless magnificent apartments, and a fine chapel, comprise this celebrated *château*. One of the objects most worthy of admiration is its armoury. Coats of mail, barbed steeds, shields, helmets, cross-bows, and weapons of every description, wrought and inlaid in a curious manner, form the riches of this ancient treasury of heroes. In short, turn where we would, we could see no want of any furniture or appendage which ought to belong to the age of chivalry, to a castle once the princely residence of the most renowned warriors of Spain.

Its situation is deserving of the structure. The view from the height on which these proud towers stand commands a luxuriant plain, even to the horizon! The smooth waves of the Esla are seen intermingling their meandering line of liquid light with the deep shade of the woods; which spread their *verdant* majesty to the base of the distant hills. But even there the sight is not bounded, for the snow-shrouded mountains afar, from their throne of clouds overlook the blue summits of the nearer heights, commixing their heads with the visionary forms of heaven.

To the inhabitant of flat countries the sublime painting of Ossian, and the wonderful descriptions of the old romance, are deemed not only poetical but absurdly extravagant. These readers cannot understand the grey ghost of a warrior in his robe of mist meeting his sons in their morning hunt upon his native mountains;—the airy castle appearing to woo the wayfaring knight to shelter, and then vanishing at once amidst a sweep of clouds. All these are passing strange; are wild, unnatural vagaries in the apprehension of a stationary resident of the plains. But take him to the highlands of Scotland, or bring him to the mountains of Spain, and he will meet the spirits of heroes in the blast; and see castellated towers ravished from sight, and restored again by the floating genii of the air.

After the exquisite feast of antiquity I had enjoyed in the castle of Beneventè, sorry was I to find that two regiments besides artillery were quartered amid such invaluable remains. These superb saloons lodged several hundreds of a rank of warriors very different from the bannered heroes who used to doff *cuirasses* here a century or two ago. Little respect is ever shewn by the lower orders of any profession to the relics of past times—to the finest specimen of arts with which they have no acquaintance. And therefore it is not so wonderful as it is lamentable; that, like their brethren in degree and necessity, the privates of our armies see no good in anything that does not administer to their wants: Alas, poor Beneventè! how soon wast thou robbed of all thy proud array! how soon were thy regal halts reduced to the ruin which is ever the marks of a retreating army!

That, such devastation is highly blameworthy is true; and the officers literally lamented it in dust and ashes; for there was sufficient of both spread over the desolated castle: but to prevent it was beyond their power. When almost every man is of one mind, nothing less than a miracle, can compel them to obey perhaps two or three individuals who command in a direction opposite to the general will.

Much as we must abhor this destroying propensity, a palliation, though no apology, may be offered for the manner in which our troops treated the unoffending furniture of Beneventè.—The offence then taken against the Spaniards;—a sense of having been allured into the country by false promises of support—of having been betrayed into disadvantageous positions—of having been abandoned to the enemy, and forced by such desertion to relinquish a victory, and retreat where they expected to conquer: all these things excited an indignation in their breasts which, perhaps, luckily for the people we were amongst, wreaked itself on their chairs and tables instead of on their heads.

Several old and large churches add to the dignity of this city; but it possesses no square of any magnitude; and the streets are in the usual Spanish fashion, very narrow and very inconvenient. A double rampart of stone and mud walls well strengthened with towers encircle the town, and complete its warlike appearance. Such is the quality of our present entertainment. The halls of reception, you will say, I have described; but nowhere the banquets!—Very true, my friend; and that I may continue to speak truth, the least that is said on so scanty a subject, the better. Therefore *adieu!*

Villa Franca, January 1809.

Towards the afternoon of the day following our arrival at Benevente, when the rear of our army had marched in, an alarm was given that the enemy were on the opposite heights.

All was on the alert in a moment: artillery, wagons, guns, and troops of every description, were hastening to their points of rendezvous. Cavalry were pouring out of the narrow gates of the city; and not a creature existed within the walls but was in motion. The plain beneath was spotted with monks and other fugitives flying in all directions, to avoid the approaching enemy; whilst the poor terrified women that remained in the bustling streets were crying and sobbing at every corner. Our information was true: but the French seeing we were not unprepared, merely looked at us from the heights and retired.

Previous to this alarm, we had decided that the bridge crossing the river should be destroyed; and now, that we found the enemy so very near, a party of the staff corps, with, I believe, one officer of engineers, were sent forth to prepare for its destruction. The houses on its opposite bank were burnt; the port fire was lighted, and the fine arches of this, ancient fabric were soon torn asunder. The explosion had effected what we wished; and the progress of the French seemed to be so far arrested. Part of our army marched out, and the remainder of the infantry were to be on the wing the following morning.

The demolishing of the bridge took place on the 29th of December, about daybreak: in about an hour or two afterwards, the French cavalry again appeared on the heights; and to our infinite surprise we saw them pressing the river about three hundred yards below the ruins of our explosion.

At this juncture the whole of our infantry and heavy artillery had departed. Sir John Moore was still in the town, as well as were Lord Paget and General Stewart, with their cavalry. The piquets were instantly ordered out. The Third Germans were the first who formed; and charged the enemy on his gaining the Benevente bank of the Esla. The remainder of our piquets coming up, seconded the bravery of this corps; and the French fell on all sides beneath the sabres of our gallant fellows, and the weight of their fine horses. This body of the enemy's cavalry was composed of five squadrons of the Life Hussars of Napoleon, and were under the command of a general of division called Le Febre. Whilst the victory continued doubtful, which was bravely contested by our adversary, we brought up two pieces of horse-artillery, stationed them near the bridge, and opened; a well-directed fire on the French, who now gave way, and attempted to retire across the ford.

For the number engaged on either side nothing could be more honourable to both than the intrepidity and firmness of this little action. But British steadiness at length prevailed; and the French taking to the water, the struggles of the wounded and dying, who even in this state took to flight and plunged into the waves; the separated parties still scattered on the shore, engaging man to man, with their eager pursuers, and falling in heaps under the strokes of their arms: these various situations formed such a striking scene that, had Loutherbourg or Sir Francis Bourgois been on the spot, they must have brought away a memorial of one of the finest skirmishes that ever was fought.

We took about one hundred prisoners, with some officers of rank, and Le Febre, their colonel. But more than double that number must have been the return of their slain. The loss we sustained was trifling. Our wounded did not exceed thirty men; and an officer of the Third German was the only person of that rank which suffered in this affair. It may be expected that the enemy, having so grievously felt the superiority of those who cover our retreat, will henceforward keep at a more respectful distance. Rumour has told us, that. Buonaparte was on the heights during this battle.

For our honour, I wish he had been; but for his own, I cannot believe it to be true; He never would have stood there inactively beholding the destruction of some of his finest troops, but must have descended to the plain, and then our gallant commander might have had the pleasure of measuring words with the mighty dictator of nations. At least, if this proud bird of Jove disdained to honour a few British hussars with his august presence in the affray, he would have sent forth a parent's eye from his eyrie on the cliff, and launched some thunderbolts to rescue from our grasp so many eaglets of his valiant nest.

Having refreshed our feverish temples, with these new laurels bound round our brows, we advanced towards Abeneza, a distance of five leagues, and halted there that night. And being anxious to lose no time in reaching a country better adapted to our circumstance, we did not linger there, but early next morning recommenced our march, and proceeded to Astorga. This was the rendezvous of our army; and here we almost all met. Besides our own troops, we were joined by five thousand fugitives, the remain of the Marquis de la Romana's force, who had fled hither on hearing of the enemy's approach to Leon. We find that the French entered that city on the 30th of December.

Astorga bears the usual character of Spanish towns. It is strongly encompassed by a high stone wall, and many towers, which at a little distance appear like a castle; but on a nearer view the mistake is discovered and you perceive them to be only planted at certain points along the wall, giving both strength and magnificence to this striking style of rampart. The gates which lead into the city are of the same warlike character, and are richly ornamented. The interior of the place is tolerably fair.

According to the necessary plan of all the ancient fortified towns, the streets are narrow, but they possess a respectable market-place, and a great church, which is a very fine building. The holy animation of the place cannot be inconsiderable, if we may judge of its devotion by the number of priests. I never, no not even all the while I was in Salamanca, saw such multitudes of ecclesiastics as here I met in one day.

The ensuing morning, at a good hour, we once more moved off, halting at a village called Bembeberes. Hitherto all had been plain but now the face of nature began to alter its features. The level gradually assumed a more swelling line; hills rose before us; and the valleys deepening their bed, we proceeded along paths whose mountainous sides presented the wildest and most romantic varieties from the luxuriant cultivation through which we passed. So beautiful, so harmonious was the scene of our march! But the actors in it exhibited a rather discordant tone.

During this part of our campaign I found that much discontent existed with the officers of our different regiments respecting: provisions: but while they murmured amongst themselves, only complaints were loudly preferred by the men, remonstrating against their want of everything necessary to support life under so laborious and harassing a march.

Situated as we were, these evils, as far as they depend on our leader, were hardly to be avoided. Retreating in so numerous a multitude, and all confined to the same road without the option of choosing another (so closely were we pressed by the enemy), was one cause of our present straits. The produce of the country had already been almost wholly devoured by the French: judge then how difficult it would be to provide, even in the barest manner, provisions sufficient to subsist so large a body. And when we add to this failure at the very source, the waste which is occasioned by the turbulent conduct of the soldiers themselves, you will not be surprised that one half of the army should be entirely without food.

It is to be lamented that the officers have not applied themselves to remedy this evil, by seeing that the men receive their rations in an orderly manner. The non-commissioned officers are at these times of no avail; no respect is paid either to their remonstrances or commands; and the men crowd to the doors of the different houses, where wines, &c. are to be given out; and with the most impatient and tumultuous vehemence demand their supply. Not waiting to be served in proper rotation, they force their way into the place, helping themselves, and destroying in their haste half what was prepared for those who were to follow; oversetting the wine, trampling on everything, and terrifying the affrighted native, whose charge it was to dispense the provisions, until, for his own safety's sake, he makes the best of his way from amongst such a herd of unrestrainable and violent men.

This, with many other instances of the like nature, mark the wide difference between a retreating and an advancing army. In the one case, all is hope, spirit, and honour. In the other, disappointment, dejection, and anticipated contempt, entirely change the man, and make him incur the very obloquy he fears. Retreat is never an agreeable movement at the best; and when at the worst, as it is with us, no fancy can imagine its misery, no pen describe its horrors.

At Benevente an order had been issued to assure the army that Corunna was not the object of our falling back; but that our march was only to secure a more favourable position. No asseverations could make the soldiery believe this: it was too evident by all our movements that Corunna was our destination; that it was an absolute retreat! and the wide disappointments they had met, drove them to despair. Worn out with fatigue and hope delayed, they no longer seemed to value life, nor any of its regulations; sufficient for them was it to snatch the hasty morsel of the day; for the next morning might see each individual on the causeway a breathless corpse.

Every object which presented itself on the roads and in the villages were so many proofs of the terrors of war, and of the devastation that surrounded us. Famishing peasantry fled by us with gaunt and horrid looks; while; as we marched along we passed their kindred of all ages; dying and dead, without power to relieve them, or to rescue our own followers from a similar fate. But it was not enough that our track should be strewed with the expiring bodies of our fellow-creatures: the poor animals, who had supported our way-worn frames, who had dragged our baggage from steep to steep, fell exhausted on the earth, and in countless, numbers heaped the sides of the road. In short, not a day, not an hour passed without adding some new calamity to our distress and wretchedness.

The army in no respect seemed the remains of the same we had brought from Portugal. Its appearance, its discipline, were gone. You could not suppose that the officers it was before so ready to obey, commanded it now; all deference to their orders was lost; and it was with the greatest difficulty that we could deter the men from, not only pillaging, but committing every excess which is hardly excusable in an enemy. Even with all our exertions, we saw villages and houses burning, in all directions; some put in that condition by negligence, but many, I must say, by the wantonness of our refractory men.

The poor cottagers were plundered; and multitudes of homeless, destitute people were continually hastening to the officers as they came up, imploring them for a redress which was out of their power to bestow. Alas! our pity and regret were all we had to offer; and they retired in an anguish, the recollection of which even now wrings my soul. But it is not compassion alone which excites what is now passing in my breast; it is shame for dishonoured England—dishonoured by the indignant despair of her troops, even while her own faithful hand was opened to abundantly succour the nation in which we suffered. It is true, we have been deceived, abandoned in Spain; but the treachery or weakness of other, should be no lesson to teach us base retaliation. Every officer with the army feels in this respect as I do; and are more grieved at such misconduct in our troops than by all their other misfortunes.

So great was the terror, their violences created, these firings of houses, these plunderings of property, that we even spread a desert before us. As soon as the peasantry heard of our approach they fled; and often on our arrival in a place we found it deserted. The road leading to the town whence I now address you was covered with these unhappy fugitives, both male and female of every age. Scarcely a mile was traversed without our viewing broken down wagons, and destroyed ammunition, mingled with the carcasses of our own invaluable horses piled on each other. A little onward, we saw other groups plunging in the agonies of death; having been lamed from fatigue and want of shoeing. At the moment they fell, we were obliged to shoot them, for fear of their becoming the spoil of the enemy; or of being starved for want of a nourishment the desolated ground could no longer yield.

Thus was the scene; sad and direful enough, without any extraneous calamity; but the elements were to lend their horrors also. The pouring clouds were to throw their torrents upon the heads of our fainting troops; rendering the roads almost impassable for our mules and wheeled carriages; destroying the already tattered shoes of our soldiery; and drenching their emaciated bodies with a wet which we had no fires to dry, no alimental powers to repel.

On quitting Bembeberes, where myself and several other officers (accompanied by our horses, whom we considered as faithful friends) took up our abode in the barn of a wine-press, the country bore a very romantic aspect; and in the summer, when war is far distant from its groves and Arcadian recesses, it must afford an enchanting seclusion to those who are enamoured of nature in her garb of trees and founts, and winding streams, and gentlest beauty! The whole way from Astorga to Villa Franca the landscape is thus lovely; and often it called from my breast a sincere sigh, that ambition so troubles this earth as to call distant nations, even from the north, to stem her torrent, and to dye with their blood the flower-enamelled southern plains.

We are now at Villa Franca; I must here drop my pen. I dare not tell you of the dreadful objects that lie before me as I look from my window: they are enough to make one muse even to madness. But others are in prospect. The stage for many a wretched scene I see in yon distant mountains, whose pale heads we must pass over before we can rest with any security. On their cold bosoms, how many of ours may lie, never to move more! *Adieu*, dear S——! Different, far different were the letters I expected to write to you from this land of vaunted enthusiasm. Alas! that words have been given to us instead of actions! Words that have made me the recorder of disaster instead of victory. Once more farewell.

LETTER 20

Lugo, January, 1809.

I closed my last letter, my dear S——, without willing you the compliments of the season; without congratulating you on the opening of a new year, surrounded as you are by the heartfelt delights of social society, and all the cheering comforts attached to the domestic hearth. Here, we have none of them. The recollection that they once were ours is like a dream that is past. Houseless, exposed on these sterile hills, few of us can expect to taste such sweet rest again.

What we now feel, proves to me with a stronger conviction than ever, the influence of the mind over the body, either by empowering it to endure, or, by leaving the nerves unbraced, allowing it to sink in exhaustion. Even this long march, these almost impenetrable snows, these hard privations, how gladly would we have encountered them all had we been marching to the field of glory; had we been suffering for, and proceeding to, the assistance of a brave and patriotic people who were seriously determined to contend even unto death for liberty; who were sincere in their proffered friendship; who would have received us, their auxiliaries and brethren in arms, with honesty and zeal!

With such hopes, with such assurances, how would our buoyant spirits have borne up our fatigued bodies; how would the ardour of our minds have repelled the winter's cold; how would the anticipated welcome of a grateful people have touched the parched lip with a refreshing balm that is better than wine!

MOUNTAIN OF NOGALLIS

Sweet hope is the vivifying power of life; and while we had her, no slackened nerve, no dejected countenance, no whisper of discontent was known in our ranks; but now she is withdrawn, the mind is robbed of its impulse of its aim.

Enthusiasm led us hither; a wide victory was our object: while it seemed before us, our eager souls, eagle-like, flew onward as towards the sun. But when we turn round; when all this is abandoned; when we are to cross the vast plains of Spain, and to climb its almost inaccessible mountains, to retreat—what must be our thoughts? Disappointment at present; condolence in the end!—And thus the lately active and spirited soldier is transformed into the heavy unmanageable follower. A sad and direful change! I cannot bear to dwell upon it.

If I recollect right, you left me last gazing on the towering heights of snow which we were soon to tread; and which, thank God, we have now passed over. The horrid scenes I anticipated I have witnessed; but they are past: and I hope that no future hours of our melancholy journey are destined to bring before me such racking spectacles of misery and death.

We left Villa Franca on the 2nd; exploring a wild and pictur-esque valley, through which the road continued along the side of the river, till it gradually ascended and brought us on the acclivity of those mountains over which we were to march, and in whose gelid bosom we were to lie that night. I cannot with sufficient colouring of language describe the romantic sublim-ity of the scenery which parted on each side as we pursued our way, till we entered upon regions which caused us, to bid it a final *adieu*, and seemed to open before us a trackless eternity of winter. We had only one pathway; and that formed in the precipitous steep, wound up the mountain to its bleak summit, and crossing this rendezvous of all the storms, runs with a deep descent into the vale beneath.

The entrance to this pass might certainly have been well de-fended. But it was not our object at this moment to take up a military position: at least it would not have been this, where no means of supply existed. And if necessity enforced us to dispute any part of the ground, the avenue on the opposite side would be so much better, as we should have a country in our rear where we could keep open a chance of receiving supplies from Corunna. But nothing appeared in our movements indicative of a stand being intended to be made at all between this and the coast; as Sir John Moore, while we were at Villa Franca, to facilitate our march, had ordered whatever magazines and carriages which he considered as more cumbersome than useful to be destroyed. Sorry was I to see that so much plumage of our wings was deemed indispensable; and that to unburthen them, such quantities of valuable ammunition were made to perish in vain.

But to the particulars of our march. We left our commanders in the town. The artillery and head-quarters proceeding first, leaving General Baird's column, and the cavalry under Lord Paget, to cover out rear, and to keep off the enemy, who were rather too close. However, whenever they were rash enough to attack us, they paid dearly for their temerity; and found that our retreat had barbs in its tail that stung even unto death. At Calcavallas the dragoons and rifle corps most gallantly checked the career of the French, and added another fresh leaf to our drooping laurels. Withering as they were, their gloom bore no proportion to the sad cypress which at every step overhung our path.

What I had before witnessed on our march was but a faint sketch of what I was yet to see in the full horrors of death and desolation. We were now in the heart of a stupendous country cleft into abyss-like ravines, and overlaid with a deep and trackless snow. Thus did the month of January, 1809, close, as well as open a miserable new year on thousands. Brought into regions, in many parts above the clouds, with no provisions to sustain nature, no shelter to shield us momentarily from the storm, no fuel to warm us, no safe spot where on to linger for an instant to rest; but all one waste of severest winter. Imagine such a place; then think of the other disasters incidental to war. The sick and wounded dragged over these immeasurable tracks; the beasts which draw their wagons failing at every step, and they left to perish in the snows, or to fall into the hands of the enemy.

I shall never forget the horrors of these dreadful days. The field of battle is a festival of honour; a sublime pageant: But this is war! Here are the red dragons yoked to her fiery car! Here are her sufferings, her woes, her wide destructions. Every yard we passed over was marked with some heart-rending proof of our miseries. Ah, little need would the French have to seek our line of march! It might be traced for many a league by our over-turned baggage, by our maimed cattle, by our dying and dead. When we had nearly gained the highest point of these slippery precipices, I looked round, and saw the rear of the army winding along the narrow road; I saw their way marked by the wretched people who lay on all sides expiring from fatigue and the severity of the cold. As their bodies reddened in spots the white surface of the ground, I could not but think on the lines of Hohenlinden:

Ah, few shall part where many, meet!
The snow shall be their winding sheet;
And every turf beneath their feet
Shall be a soldier's sepulchre!

But not so; where they fell they lay. No turf covered them from the beating elements; and as a sad memorial of our betrayed cause, their bones lie on the mountains of Spain, an everlasting reproach to her ungrateful sons.

I observed amongst the unfortunates a Portuguese bullock driver. He was on his knees amidst the snow, with his hands clasped, breathing forth a prayer for his soul. This poor fellow had attended us from the first day of our march, and, thus faithful to our service, expired. I was a very few paces from him when his last groan pierced my ears. Near him lay a woman, half enveloped in a blanket, the wife of a soldier; she was also cold in death. A little infant, yet living, was hanging at the breast of its inanimate mother, vainly endeavouring to find that warmth and nourishment which fate had for ever withdrawn.

Were I to enumerate every afflicting object which met my view during this dreadful mountain march, I should fill a volume instead of a sheet; I should unman your heart, and send my reader weeping from the tale. But one more I will repeat, and then for a short time, at least, *adieu* to these narrations.

In winding round the road (which was bounded the whole way with terrific precipices) at the turning of an angle rather more sheltered than the rest from the iron-icy sleet that tore along the sloping ravines, we saw the body of a woman lying in a situation, that for misery, while she was sensible to its horrors, must have been unequalled. She was dead; and two little babes, to which she had just given birth, lay struggling in the snow. The scene was too agonizing to bear a second glance. A blanket thrown over her soon hid her from our sight; and we had the satisfaction of seeing the poor infants given in charge to a woman who came up in one of the bullock carts.

A continuation of these spectacles opened upon us all the way to Lugo, and doubly proved the reasonableness of my former objections against women being the followers of an army into hostile scenes. If men find it hard to bear the fatigues of a severe campaign, how must women sink under them! And if men find them insupportable, what must be the dreadfully varied fate of the feebler sex! No wonder that the corpses of these unhappy females strew our path, when our bravest fellows fall faint and incapable of further exertion.

Two battles could hardly have cost us more men than I fear we shall find missing when we have leisure to enumerate our loss. The ascent of this mountain will have deprived us of thousands, besides the dead left on the way; for those who yet survive and lie on the road must, in their defenceless state, surrender to the enemy. The darkness of a Cimmerian winter-night veiled these dismal pictures from our eyes: and we continued our weary route in a silence which was alone interrupted by the howlings of the blast, or the dying groans of our dropping companions.

At last we arrived at what was denominated a village; but it was almost buried in the snow, and with some difficulty a few of us made our way under shelter. Even so slight a comfort was comparative heaven. I, with my party, got into a poor hovel, and lighting a fire (our only refreshment, for provisions we had none), laid ourselves around it, placing our horses to enjoy it in an outer circle, till the dawn summoned us to advance and again rolled up the dark curtain of fate.

We now began to descend the tremendous pass, crossing several bridges, which we immediately attempted to destroy with the hope of impeding the approach of our enemy; but an evil genius seemed to thwart all our efforts. Every exertion that was made to compass their destruction failed; and thus all facility was left to smooth the passage of the French in their pursuit.

On the 4th we arrived at Lugo, where we shall remain to give time for our stragglers who are able to come up; and, I suppose, we shall here settle some plan for a division of our force; part to march to Vigo, and part to Corunna. At present, our numbers increase our distress.

Amongst the minor misfortunes which attended our hard pressed ascent up this terrible mountain was the necessity we found ourselves in to disencumber the march of a considerable weight of dollars. Unable to conceal them, we were obliged to hurl them into the adjacent valley. The means of transporting them farther had failed; the animals which had drawn them, fell down dead on the road; and as many thousands of horses and mules shared the same fate, to find any to supply their place was now impossible. The close pursuit of the French did not allow us time to distribute them amongst the officers and men; hence no alternative was left but to commit them to the bosom of the snow. There, I hope, they will be buried till the departure of the present wintry shroud unveils to some lucky peasantry this mine of silver.

The same reason that prevailed with us to sacrifice this wealth, also compelled us to abandon about seventy or eighty Spanish wagons filled with clothes, shoes, &c. for the use of the nation; all which we brought from England, and all which must now fall into the hands of our enemies. A hundred patriots we left as their guard; but I have no doubt that they, as well as their charge, are now in possession of the French, who must have come up with them on the second of this month, about a couple of leagues on this side of Villa Franca.

We have now taken up a position on a line of hills between three and four miles from Lugo, where our head quarters are, and consequently where I am stationed. Happy, you may be sure, we are to have arrived at a place of temporary repose. This city, in more honourable times to Spain, was once its metropolis; but now it is inferior to many of the provincial towns we have lately passed through; however, its fine encircling walls, towers, and gates, testify its ancient consequence, and frown sternly on its present totally defenceless and ruined state.

A large church, and a palace, the residence of a bishop, ornament it streets. Two or three convents, besides hospitals, rearing their spires in the air, and considerably to the dignity of the view. A large square and a fountain finish the *agrémens* of Lugo. The avenues leading to this antiquated metropolis, as well as the gates, are narrow in the extreme; and the dirt and rain still farther impeding our entrance into them, you will not wonder that we were much slower in egress than in wishes; and that wearied out with fatigue and watching, we sunk down in the first shed to life-reviving sleep.

Here then do we await the arrival of our reserve and cavalry. The brigades of Generals Crawford and Alton have proceeded towards Vigo, and are followed by the division under General Frazer; consequently our part are determined to seek Corunna. In the word Corunna, of course, we must include that of exit from this perilous scene; and if we are to fare no better than we have hitherto done, having been most impressively wooed into Spain, and as shamefully jilted when there, we must look on the sight of the ocean our own empire, and on the proud vessels our best fortresses, as the very havens of Providence, prepared for our refuge from the weakness of our allies and threatened dishonour. Nothing but re-embarkation can now be expected as our object.

We cannot but particularly regret, in the midst of such general supineness, the apathy to our situation and to their own ultimate benefit which seems to enchain the Galicians. Although many of them have shewed themselves to us from the mountain tops in arms; and well aware as they are of the use they might be in covering our retreat; yet no exertion has been attempted on their part to arrest the progress of the French even for a moment: such an effort could easily have been made from their knowledge of these their native bulwarks; and its. success would most probably have been commensurate with their zeal.

Deserted as we had been in the first instance by the boasting patriots of Spain; yet, I must confess, that on seeing these men with muskets, &c, prowling about in large bodies amongst the heights, we took it for granted they had turned out to support us, and that we should soon hear of their making some signal attempt to impede the march of our enemies; but these our natural expectations were soon silenced by the event. These valiant Galicians, these redoubted patriots, were only leaving their homes that they might not assist us; having previously secreted everything which might have been rendered serviceable, and driven away their mules and oxen into the distant fastnesses, whither themselves were now eagerly hastening.

When we arrived at these deserted dwellings, we found no remnant of bread for ourselves, not a straw for our famishing cattle; and not a beast to replace even one of the vast multitudes we had unavailingly lost in their service. Our draft animals and baggage mules having almost all perished, and no means of recruiting them arising, we were consequently obliged (dreadful necessity!) to relinquish many carts full of the sick and fatigued, as well as others laden with necessaries, to the hard chance of falling into the grasp of our inveterate foe.

Our position is ably taken up; and every instant our poor stragglers are coming in; but as provisions, scanty at the first, are running famishingly low, I fancy our halt will not be for many hours longer, During this repose I write these hasty narratives of our movements, and shall address you again at my next leisure moment. Meanwhile, farewell.

LETTER 21

Corunna, January, 1809.

Famine, pestilence, and death are said to be three furies ever attendant on war! We have found the remark a just one: for having encountered famine and death in almost every shape, this part of the land is now threatened with a direful pestilence. We have been the secondary causes of this impending plague; but the people who misled us into the situation, being the origin of our accumulated evils, they are certainly the primary causes of all these dismal consequences.

Our cavalry and the artillery horses on entering this city were found in such a state of debility and irremediable lameness from the want of shoes, that many fell dead in the streets, and more were obliged to be shot in mercy to their sufferings.

The streets, the grand square, and *piazzas* are now filled with their putrefying bodies. Horrible is the sight, and more horrible is the sound, for not a minute of the day is permitted to elapse without our hearing the report of some pistol or musket depriving these once noble creatures of life. The heavy rains have swollen and burst many of the carcasses; and the infected air hovers so rancorously about our heads, that it is almost impossible to pass in any direction without feeling violent convulsions of stomach, and prognosticating all the calamitous effects of imbibed putrefaction.

Should we escape as from only a short sojourn here we probably may, I cannot calculate on a similar good fortune befriend-

CORUNNA

ing the natives of the town. They will be left to the full effluvia of more than 400 lifeless horses and mules; and must of course respire in every breath all the diseases which a death-tainted atmosphere engenders.

After this enforced slaughter of our faithful quadruped friends, we soon foresaw work of a more congenial description. Owing to our failure in the destruction of the bridges, the enemy advanced rapidly upon us, and appearing in sight, accumulated in great strength on a good position opposite to the ground we had chosen. A valley divided the two armies; each of course possessing the road leading through their separate lines.

On the 6th our outposts were attacked. The dismounted *chasseurs a cheval* of the enemy advanced, and a couple of Spanish pieces of ordnance (one of which was a howitzer) they had taken on their march, opened upon us. They assaulted us with great spirit; but at that moment the depressed souls of our men seemed suddenly to revive; every arm was braced; the shock was received with a steadiness that excited even our own wonder; and the impetuous assailants were repulsed with much loss, while we were scarcely deprived of a man.

On the 7th our foe rallied, and again came forward with redoubled force. But our second reception was equal to our first; his charge was met with resistless gallantry; and rolling him back upon his ranks, we drove them before us into the narrow lines; filling the path with those men killed and wounded, whose eager onset had been cheeked by our bayonets, and whom we now laid in a bloody graves.

During this affair nothing could exceed my admiration, of the conduct of our men, but the transcendent courage, coolness, and steadiness of our officers. All seemed like a race started from the dead. The moment they heard the shout of battle, their ardour burst forth as if they had never known despondence, never felt fatigue. The poor drooping individual who the instant before was lagging along the road; and leaning on any accidental support, as if to sustain him a moment from the death to which he was sinking,—no sooner heard that an attack was to be made, than springing from the earth, forgetting his misery, and newly inspired with life, his strong sinews grasped his ready bayonet, and he pressed forward to join his party or regiment now hot in the contest.

It was a sight that filled every officer with redoubled animation; and as we felt our power and saw its effects, we could not but turn with greater indignation to a people for whom we were fighting, and who, leaving us without common resources, had despoiled our brave fellows of the opportunities for glory they came to seek, and our commanders of the fame which, when untrammelled, has ever been their due.

In these actions I saw the demonstration of my opinion respecting the recent disorder of our men. It was despair; it was all that makes a soldier hold down his head and forget his responsibility to military law, indeed to any law. But now that honour again presented herself, each man fell into his line of duty; every man became obedient, and as ready to submit to the strictest discipline as when in the fullest tide of success, in the ample enjoyment of every hope and every comfort.

In the second encounter we took a considerable number of prisoners, and killed many of the enemy. One only of our officers was wounded, Brigade-Major Roberts, a brave veteran, whose right hand was carried away by a shot, but not until he had gallantly buried the point which it held repeatedly in the hearts of those whose bayonets threatened him on all sides.

We took more prisoners this day than in the preceding affair; and from them we learnt that large reinforcements had arrived to the enemy; under the command of General Soult. Consequently a third and heavier attack was to be expected; and with every necessary precaution, Sir J. Moore prepared for the event.

The division under General Frazer was recalled from the Vigo road, and accordingly marched towards our position.

The artillery and the cavalry were placed in order on the morning of the 8th; by dawn we were all under arms, and the whole army present were drawn out to offer battle. That sun appeared which we expected would set in blood; it rose in storms, and a tremendously tempestuous day it proved; but, alas! it was only with the elements that we fought! Soult either did not conceive himself sufficiently strong to warrant his quitting his favourable position to come down and attack us, or his object was not to bring us to a decisive fight; for he must have known our miserable state with regard to supplies, and therefore left us to be defeated by the surer means of delay and disappointment.

It was our commander's wish that we should be attacked on the morning of the 8th. He was well-assured that every man would do his duty; and more than hoped that in consequence of that the enemy would be so incapacitated as to allow us to get such start of them as would enable us to embark without molestation.

It was not in our power, nor was it our interest, to assault General Soult. In the first place his position was excellent; and, secondly, his force was superior. However, from the break of day, until the gloom of evening shrouded our enemies from our view, we waited their attack. To linger longer in this expectation would have been very imprudent; therefore, when night came on, fires were lighted along our line; and thus deceiving our adversaries with a show of remaining; stationary, we prepared for removal.

Had we been masters of any resource for, the subsistence of the army, our greatest evil must have vanished, and Sir John Moore would have kept his sword extended as long as General Soult chose to stand at lock: but as we were situated, retreat was our only alternative.

Under the screen of our friendly fires, which lighted us on our way, and beguiled, the French, to think we still remained stirring them, we again turned our course towards Corunna.

The bow was once more unbent; and on, the 10th, Betanzas beheld our sad and disjointed divisions, by brigades and regiments arrive; and a melancholy scattered and dreadfully dying march it was. Groups, similar to the pale and lifeless heaps we had left on the precipices of the Nazalles mountains, again marked our starving and desolate advance. Amongst the number who fell, died a poor woman I mentioned to you in a former letter as having seen walking from Salamanca with her new-born babe in her arms; and at this last exertion, fatigue and misery overcame her, and she expired ere we entered Betanzas.

Of course no longer time was allowed here than was necessary for the gathering in of the scattered troops, and to form them into a more condensed body. This done, we pushed off towards Corunna; and after paving the roads with our exhausted fellow soldiers, who, dropping down, begged, as the last favour we could grant, to be left to die—we arrived on the 11th at the wished-for port.

Happy were we to see the walls, even from a distance, that promised some boundary to our miseries. We had experienced all the evils of the direst campaign without any of its rewards. We had suffered, fought, and endured every privation. But a cross destiny, or rather the perverse mismanagement of those who sat at the helm in Spain, had robbed us of a soldier's best mede—honour and glory.

I shall never forget the agitating joy which burst from the swelling hearts of the advancing columns when they ascended the hill which presented a view of the ocean and the British ships that were then riding its waves. We all could have shouted as if we had beheld a deity; the gracious protector that was to snatch us from the grasp of our enemy! Our proud vessels seemed to bear the sword of retribution; secure in the prospect of being soon under their flag, every fainting bosom beat with renewed ardour, and looking towards their swelling sails as they bounded forwards, our slackened swords were again grasped in our hands; and, like the returning prodigal son revisiting his home, we anticipated restrung nerves, and a trial of strength with our proud foe, on some more faithful and propitious shore.—*Adieu!*

LETTER 22

Corunna, January, 1809.

My last to you, dear S——, contained the consolatory information that we had, at length, reached the wished-for port, It was on the 11th of this month; and had the transports been come round from Vigo we should have embarked without molestation; our rapid march after our rejected offer of battle to Soult having given us greatly the advantage, in advance, before our enemies. But our brave fellows seem fated to disappointment! The particular vessels we expected to meet were yet far away; and hemmed in between the sea and our accumulating foe, we were destined to await the issue.

Our general has taken up a position in front of Corunna; the best he could have assumed, in order to watch the coming in of the transports, and to cover our embarkation when we are fortunate enough to hail their arrival.

The French have overtaken us: our means to impede them have failed; one of which was the destruction of the bridge of Burgo, that crossed the Rio de Burgo; but, on the ebbing of the tide, the water became fordable, and our ever-watchful enemies, taking advantage of the circumstance, are now in front of us, hourly increasing their numbers, and incessantly annoying our troops. They occupy the high ground before us with their right extending across the great road,

Thus then, in sight of each other, are we stationed; and whether we shall be obliged to dispute the little land now left between us and the sea I know not; but if they attempt to drive us into its waves, according to the proud declarations of their Imperial chief, I trust we will none of us stir a step; that not one individual will shrink from the spot, though it prove his grave, determining to conquer or to die, but never to yield an enforced possession.

However, as the enemy seem yet to eye us with the cautious glances of jealousy, should the transports soon arrive, I do not doubt but that, even now, we might embark with little loss, provided the elements do not also wage war against our poor remains.

We have another circumstance in our favour; the patriotic spirit and friendly activity of the governor and citizens of Corunna. They are resolved to render us every possible assistance; although they must be aware that in the case of our leaving the place free for the French to enter, their aids to us will be repaid by our enemies by consequences too terrible for anticipation to dwell on. When I think of what may be their fate, the noble ardour I admire deepens my regrets for them, and doubly arouses my indignation against their countrymen, who, by abandoning us to this extremity, have devoted some of the best Spaniards in the kingdom to almost inevitable destruction. Such is the effect of disunion; such the issue of political intrigues; such the sacrifices which individual interest makes of public welfare!

The whole city of Corunna is in one uninterrupted bustle; the streets are filled with our troops; the inhabitants, both male and female, transporting cannon and ammunition to the walls; and all the tradesmen are armed, doing duty at the gates in conjunction with our own troops.

This town, now so momentous a place to us, is situated at the foot of a range of heights, and is built on a peninsula. Nature has accommodated it with a very fine harbour on the one side, and an extensive bay (called Orson Bay) on the other.

The town is regularly and neatly built; having a very fine row of houses looking into the harbour, and commanding a magnificent view towards the coast of Ferrol. Corunna occupies the neck of land which divides the bays; and the ground gradually rising, is covered by the citadel; a work on which much expense and time has been bestowed. This august fabric, as is also the castle of St. Antonio, is built on a rock at the entrance of the harbour; and yields a good protection from marine attacks: but were we to abandon our present position and retire into the city, it would not be tenable an hour.

In the citadel are several churches and chapels, as well as the governor's residence, and those of several *grandees*. A theatre, also, enlivens its embattled walls: at least, its gay architecture reminds us of more tranquil times, when Thalia sported on the lap of peace; but now the comic troop have given place to our soldiers who are quartered in it; and more serious scenes are perhaps destined to be exhibited on its boards.

When the army of General Baird landed here, gaiety of every description bade them welcome. Plenty greeted them from all sides, and the joyful inhabitants opened their houses and their hearts to their defenders. Balls and fêtes were given; and the drama represented patriotic pieces in unison with the united zeal of England and Spain, and with the brilliant hopes which were expected to crown the coalition.

What a change do we behold! Houses abandoned; the once smiling faces of the women bathed in tears; and every prospect of want, with all the miseries that war and massacre can bring, rising in bloody apprehensions before their almost frantic senses.

Certainly, if they, in common with the generality of people, when overpowered by adverse circumstances, suppose that the misfortunes of their auxiliaries more rapidly precipitate the horrors which are pending over them; their present exertions to assist our embarkation, and determination to defend the place till our ships are out of the reach of shot is truly great, and deserves our gratitude and universal admiration. Had all Spain been sincere, zealous, and resolute as the people of Corunna, we should not have been a retreating army; and the standards of Ferdinand would now have been waving from the extremest western frontier to the eastern tops of the far distant Pyrenees.

But the vile selfishness of individuals has ruined a cause which involved the fate of Europe.

The tide is past that might have borne us on to a victory that turns the head giddy to contemplate: and now, I fear, the patriotism that remains must struggle in shallows and disappointments till it be finally overwhelmed; I grieve particularly for the noble inhabitants of Corunna; for past instances too clearly shew what is the reward their magnanimity will receive from the French conqueror. Not so the conduct of the great generals of old, when the bravery of an enemy, and their patriotic heroism called for respect, and received it from the victor. Every spark of this noble fire, every bond which by a generous union of spirit proclaimed even illustrious foes to be brethren in soul, is now lost in the torrents of blood which an ambitious individual has bid flow to dye his imperial robes in tenfold depths of purple.

Destructions of incalculable desolation precede and follow him; and as one proof of the means we have been obliged to have recourse to, even to deprive ourselves that we may not enrich him, I shall mention a circumstance which occurred this day whilst I was riding towards the outposts. All of a sudden the earth seemed to tremble beneath my horse's feet; and in an instant two explosions, the most terrible and loud I ever heard, rent the air. They were followed by a column of smoke that rose gradually to an immense height in the sky, and then overspreading the clear ether with volumes of rolling darkness. At first I believed it to be an earthquake; but the latter effect undeceived me: and as soon as my animal recovered its fright, and I my surprise, I proceeded towards the point whence the smoke issued, and there learnt its cause.

Two magazines of gunpowder had been found. The powder had been sent from England for the use of the patriots; but like our other presents of arms, clothing, &c. had been allowed to remain unappropriated. The *junta* of this district, like those of some other provinces, was so inert, or so blind to their true interest, as to leave it here useless to the patriots; but a very rich *depôt* for the invaders, whose lynx-eyes would soon have discovered its value, and whose active hands would not have lost a moment in applying it to its warlike purpose.

To prevent this event, as soon as our commanders discovered

these magazines, orders were issued for their destruction; and an artillery-officer was deputed to the management of the duty.

The gunpowder had been deposited in two buildings near a village. In the lesser edifice I am told there was between four and five thousand barrels; and in the larger eight thousand. The Spanish officer who had the care of them, reported that the great magazine was empty.

Not supposing it possible that a falsehood would be told on such a subject, our officer believed him; and this villainous Spaniard would have allowed our artillery men to have proceeded to the destruction of the small magazine totally unprepared for the horrible effects which must have ensued by the unexpected and consequent blowing up of the other. But a peasant seeing what was going forward, came up to our men, and solemnly assured them that the larger building was also full of powder.

Upon this information an application was instantly made to the Spanish officer for the key of the great magazine. He refused to yield it; and on the strength of the countryman's information we forced the door. His words were found too true. It was filled to the very top with gunpowder. No time was lost. The villagers were warned from its vicinity. The arrangements were made, the *fusees* lighted, and, at about nine o'clock, the whole blew up, roaring through the atmosphere, tearing the earth, and overwhelming everything within its influence. Not a vestige of the adjacent village was to be seen: and I fear that not a few of the infatuated inhabitants who could not be convinced of their danger, perished in the explosion.

We lost a non-commissioned officer and three or four men, that were killed by the flying fragments of the building. Few windows in the town escaped, all being broken; and the greater part of the inhabitants fell on their knees, thinking it a more serious convulsion.

Our indefatigable followers, the French, must have shared in the surprise, as they must have both heard the sound, and seen its effect. The morning was one of the finest I ever beheld. Not a cloud hovered in the heavens; not a zephyr breathed in the air; all was in a state of profound stillness; nature seemed full of peace and beauty when the horrid uproar took place; and a majestic volume of black smoke, rising in awful silence after the sudden horror of the explosion, filled the scene with an object whose sublimity was beyond description. Sublime as it was to the, eye it was much more so to the mind: and we stood gazing at it with thoughts which none who have not witnessed the like can imagine.

Awful indeed is our situation in every respect. We not only have destroyed all this ammunition, but we are putting our supernumerary horses to death. Again the incessant shot is fired, which carries a cruel fate to the hearts of these faithful animals. We have not time to embark them; and to resign them to our enemies is a sacrifice too great, policy determines, to be made to humanity. These are, indeed, the miseries of war, for they rive our hearts. Bodily anguish is much more tolerable than this sort of pain. And, therefore, to fly from their present impressions, I shall bid you a short *adieu*!

LETTER 23

At sea, Jan. 19, 1809.

Before this reaches you, no doubt you will have received better information respecting the events of the few past days than can at present be transmitted by me; although I have been on the spot, and witnessed scenes as much to the honour as to the grief of England. Long ere this meets your eye, you must be made acquainted with the general particulars of the glorious and calamitous battle of the 16th. Official communications having been yesterday dispatched to ministers at home, in a light-sailing vessel that must arrive many a day before our heavily laden transports; you may be mourning the result of our action, the details of which, though steeped in blood, would make the proud consciousness of an Englishman check his lamentations, to break forth in glorying admiration of the slain.

The images of the recent battle are too many and too prominent in my mind to allow me the power of much individualizing; but as far as my yet confused thoughts permit, I will make you still more intimate with the dauntless courage of our brothers in arms, as well as draw forth a sigh of regret for those who now lie cold on the field of death.

In my last I noted our relative situation with regard to the enemy. I think it was on the 14th that the transports from Vigo, accompanied by ten or eleven ships of war, came round. Their arrival gave us great joy, as we saw in them an asylum from all our fatigues; and every exertion was made for instant embarkation.

The artillery, a few horses, and our useless people, were put on board first. This we accomplished with ease ; and as the enemy did hot advance a foot of ground, but rested their hopes of annoying us in a range of guns which they had opened upon us, but which failed to affect our present movements, we proceeded quietly with our embarkation; having before secured all the points on this side, from which the enemy, had they seized them, might have distressed us.

On the 15th, our ever watchful adversary received considerable reinforcements; and on the morning of the following day, by certain movements on their right, we could plainly see that something was meditating to prevent our easy departure.

Our right was upon the village of Elvena, and under the command of the gallant Baird. A strong column of the enemy, covered by several pieces of the artillery which opened from an adjacent wood to the right of the village, opposed this force. For a short time this point of attack seemed to be the grand object of the French. To force our right was their aim; and the weight of the tremendous column falling at once upon our brave fellows, was enough to have struck terror into any hearts but those of Englishmen.

The brigade of Lord William Bentinck poured a well-directed fire into this concentrated mass of destruction. Three cheers from us sealed their destiny; and the bayonets of the 50th, 42nd, and 4th regiments soon completed the confusion their balls had begun. The numbers of the enemy augmented their own consternation; they fell back on each other, making a confusion as successful as our arms; and, in short, this glorious scene of valour was soon terminated by the total defeat of the column.

Not a foot of ground could the French gain in any quarter; and although fresh troops came up to the support of their discomfited brethren, they were all forced to retire.

The village, of course, became the next field of contention; and a most severe struggle took place. But they gave way again; and being hotly pursued by our people, I am sorry to say that in this brave chase we lost our two gallant friends, Majors Stanhope and Napier. Poor Stanhope, whilst following his friend at the head of a few men, received a shot through the heart. He exclaimed, "Oh, my God!" and dropped, Napier did not long survive him. I am told that he was bayoneted by some of the enemy whilst in the act of calling on his men to follow him to the seizure of some guns near the houses. Thus did these noble friends meet their fate in one day; thus do they lie together on the field of glory; and thus for ever may deathless laurels shade them.

The 50th have suffered greatly. Indeed it is rather to be wondered at that they have not incurred more loss than they have sustained so much. Their ancient character for intrepidity and the reputation they gained at Vimeira, together with their ambition to surpass, if possible, the glories of the 42nd, precipitated this brave corps into more dangerous circumstances than perhaps strict prudence could justify. One of their own officers told me since the action, that his regiment and the 42nd could not have lost less than 250 men. Great as this may appear, yet it was trifling when compared with the essential service their enterprising courage effected in producing the success of the day. But to the field again.

During this affair General Baird lost his arm; hence we were soon deprived of the assistance of this inspiriting leader. And what still farther blighted the brilliant completion of the glorious work already begun, was the fall of our commander-in-chief! He was struck by a cannon shot, and was carried expiring off the ground. The stroke was felt by us all, and by all will ever be deplored. But, thank heaven, the blow that wounded our hearts did not paralyse them; our ardour and success at this eventful moment were in their full blaze: and although the dreadful tidings of our loss were immediately spread through our right wing, and soon made their way to the left, yet neither dismay nor grief checked our courage for an instant. Vengeance as well as victory seemed to nerve every arm, and pouring on our enemies with redoubled determination, we forced them in every point to leave us the disputed ground in testimony of our advantage.

This attack on our right being frustrated, its security from farther assaults from the fresh bodies of the enemy, was effected by the excellent conduct of Major-General Paget, who was supported by Lieutenant-General Frazer.

Our centre was the next aim of the French, but they were

equally well received as on our right wing, and as successfully repulsed. Discomfited in these several attacks, a third charge was made on our left, who were much annoyed by the French troops which had obtained possession of a village on the high road. Here again the houses became objects of dispute; and the British bayonet soon made the enemy leap from the windows, or bathe with their blood the habitations of the once peaceful inhabitants.

I believe that this gallant dislodgement of the French was achieved by the 14th Regiment, who made such havoc that the enemy retired in confusion, leaving us to advance, which we did; and occupied ground far more forward than that we had possessed before the attack.

As the day closed, our enemies drew off; and at about six o'clock in the evening the sounds of artillery and the rattling of small arms were heard no more. We had silenced the French, we had compelled them to retire; and departing like the dying martyr even amid the flames of our triumph, we prepared for embarkation.

Having collected as many of our wounded as we could discover, and sent them on board; our picquets resumed their original positions, and every preparation was made for shipping the remainder of the army. During the whole night of the 16th, this service was performing; and all, excepting the brigades under Generals Hill and Beresford, were safely embarked. On this intimation the picquets fell back; and before daylight on the seventeenth they were launched with their brave comrades in the various transports.

The enemy, not imagining that we so employed ourselves during the night, lay in profound repose; perhaps anticipating our attack upon them next morning, or meditating to retrieve their late defeat by an assault on us, backed with new reinforcements.

General Beresford had occupied the ground near St. Lucia; and General Hill kept the heights in the rear of the citadel; meanwhile the natives fulfilled their promises of exertions to facilitate our embarkation: and thus we quitted Spain with stronger convictions of its patriotism than we were allowed to preserve when we first entered it at Alcantara.

In the course of the day and night of the 17th, the two brigades of Beresford and Hill were happily afloat, and nothing seemed now wanting but the aid of the winds to waft us with our new, though bleeding wreaths, to our native shores.

When our enemies perceived that we had, accomplished our object of embarkation, and that nothing remained to dispute their passage to Corunna, they advanced and possessed themselves of high ground near St. Lucia; and at about three o'clock established a battery that commanded the harbour. This done, they opened a fire on the ships that had not yet cleared from within their reach; and directing it particularly against a transport, whose misfortune it had been to get on the rocks not far from the Castle of St. Antonio, they were answered by heavy guns from our line of battle ships; but whether with any mortal effect I know not.

Our total loss in this affair cannot at present be ascertained, as no return could be given in of the numbers killed or wounded: but I learn that many of our bravest officers have fallen; and that several of them are of that rank and experience which must double our regrets, as we lose what only time and opportunities can replace. However, while we fear we hope; for our information in yet very vague on this subject; each reporter only gathering from what he saw in the bloody neighbourhood of his own actions, or collected from the confused accounts of casual lookers on in the moment of embarkation.

You, perhaps, may have a more correct account (though under our circumstances; it is impossible you should have a perfect one), as General Hope will make every exertion to transmit a proper return to England. The command devolved on that brave officer the instant Sir John Moore and Sir David Baird were *hors de combat.*

Considering everything, our embarkation after the battle was very ably conducted; and, in addition to the impression we had made upon our enemy, we are very much indebted to our friends of the navy for the easiness of our transition from the land to the sea. It was under their guidance we moved; and all was conducted with the utmost coolness and determination.

The weather, was so adverse that we had not time to file off regularly into the different transports; hence sortie overflowed, and others set sail without a soldier on board; but had the elements been in our favour, we should have been able, from the orderly dispositions of the naval officers, &c. to have dispersed our harassed multitudes more to their own comfort as well as to our own.

In the midst of our embarkation, while all was going on quietly and with due regularity, the wind springing suddenly up, filled us with fears that should we follow our former plan we must leave our covering brigades in extreme peril. Accordingly we hurried all on board in the best manner we could. And being on board, thank God that all who survive are once more afloat; that the mutilated remains of our gallant army are returning to their country to receive the rewards and consolations due to their bravery and their sufferings!

Though the folly of the Spanish *juntas* involved us in the disasters of the campaign; though the cruellest circumstances forced us into a path of retreat manifestly against the wishes of our commander-in-chief, and repugnant to ourselves; yet still the honour of England has been preserved, the lustre of her arms are unsullied.

During our whole march the enemy never opposed us without leaving us victorious. In the field we conquered, it was the desolation of the country that compelled us to retreat; possessed of resources neither of troops, provisions, nor ammunition, had we remained in the heart of Spain, even as victors, we must have perished. Therefore, having been thus constrained to seek repose for our toils in our native land, I hope the causes of our hasty retreat will be sought where they are alone to be found; and not be laid to the account of any want of judgement in our late commander, of any want of courage in our troops.

Political jealousies and ill-advised plans, not laid in the camps, but devised elsewhere, have led our forces northward: when, after the disastrous events of the Spanish armies, and our own knowledge of the naked state of these provinces, we ought rather, in common sense, to have made a retrograde motion; and so recollected our power in the sister kingdom. When I think on all we have done, on all that has been wrested from us, not by the enemy, but by our friends and allies. I am half maddened. Without a defeat, forced to leave Spain; a victor in arms, and yet a shattered army; returning to England with unsullied honour, yet with bleeding wounds; the circumstance is new to our country: and that we should not be followed by the loud huzzas of a rescued people is bitterness to us; and must be shame to those who have thus betrayed their benefactors.

We are told that Portsmouth is to be our rendezvous. Should I have an opportunity of sending this into Plymouth as we pass, I will dispatch it, to assure you that I live *to fight another day.* And meanwhile, I bid you *adieu!*

LETTER 24

Plymouth, Jan. 1809.

My dear S——.

Once again we are on English ground! I shall not descant on the joy it gave us; for unless you had shared our miseries, and ran the risk of our perils (not merely from the sword, for with that we are ready at any time to stand a tilt with our enemies, but from the treachery of our friends), you can form no idea of our transport in once more finding ourselves amongst our own people, and in our own land.

As soon as I got on shore I put two letters in the post for you; one written at Corunna, and the other at sea. The latter ought to have been accompanied by what this contains; namely, a plan of the late victory at Corunna—and so it may justly be called; for though it was dyed deep in blood, yet from that depth of woe our brave general, even in the grasp of death, caught up drowning honour by the locks: and we have borne her weeping to his native shore, to bear testimony to the merits of her preserver, and to consecrate his monument with her immortalizing tears.

My plan of this memorable battle is as correct as I could possibly do it from the circumstances we were in during the battle; but you will find it sufficiently accurate to redouble your interest when following the events of the action through the narratives lately published in the *Gazette.*

Though I am landed at Plymouth, it is not to be finally disembarked. By a mistake our division of transports, got into this harbour; but we were under orders for Portsmouth; and since our arrival here we have received a reiteration of them, and that as soon as the wind sets fair, we are to get under weigh, and proceed without further delay to the port of our first destination. Though this committing ourselves to the waves again is no very pleasant prospect, yet as we have been allowed to throw off our Spanish incrustations here, it is a blessing so great as to quell all our murmurs; and absorbed in gratitude for present ease, we will not grumble at having a few more disagreeables to endure.

You can imagine something like the inconveniences of our voyage, when I tell you that on my landing here I had not had a change of linen for many days; nay, were I to speak all the truth, I believe I should say for weeks! You must have a remembrance of the filth of our lodgings along the Spanish roads: think then what must have been .my state so accoutred, and couped up in a transport with companions equally dirty with myself. Our appearance was far more lively than we desired; and when we sprang on shore, disrobed ourselves of our tatters, and jumped into a warm bath; nothing could exceed our joy.

It seemed to have all the effects of the immortalizing Styx on me; for, as I laved my exhausted and wretched limbs in the purifying stream, I seemed to imbibe fresh life and spirits in every plunge.—Thus cleansed from all the pollutions of the disgusting part of Spain, and covered with British linen, white as snow and sweeter than the rose, imagine my delight at finding myself once more feelingly convinced of my return to cleanliness, comfort, and to England.

After enjoying these highly necessary personal satisfactions, and a little wholesome food into the bargain, news became the next object of interest to our minds: General Hope's account of the affair of the 16th was eagerly put into our hands, and as eagerly perused. I read it with various emotions. In one part I exulted in the dauntless courage of our men, in the resistless power of their arms: in the next I saw the fall of our beloved commander.

The tribute which General Hope pays to the memory of his brother hero, is beautiful: it is true; and the soldier's heart must be of iron and not of human mould that can read it without a tear.

Gallant Moore, low art thou laid! In blood has the rays of thy fame been sunk, but not extinguished; they shoot the brighter from thine ashes, and settle on thy grave. Distant from thy native land, like the tomb of Achilles, it will hereafter become the pilgrimage of heroes, to stand where thou art laid, and with brave regrets to muse upon thy valour and thy fate!

The particulars of his death few of us accurately knew till we fell in with the persons who attended him in his last moments. How invincible was his spirit even when death was in his heart! how truly heroic were the short sentences he addressed to the officers who met him as he was borne from the field! Every word in his last conference with those. around him marked the greatness of his mind and the virtues of his heart. The patriot, the friend, the affectionate son, glowed in every sentence. The very spirit of magnanimity united with the tenderest affections beamed forth in this expiring hero with more than mortal brilliancy, and seemed to wing his soul to regions where his glories will shine for ever without a cloud.

An arm-chest received the remains of this invaluable officer: he was interred in a bastion on the right of the citadel gate, close to General Anstruther, who had been buried there but the day before. A foreign sepulchre holds their mortal part: but while the memory of man lasts, and the heights of Corunna exist to point where they lie, their monument will be in every honourable breast, and their fame be as immortal as their spirits.

The more I reflect on the events of the last few weeks, on what we were, and on what we are now, the greater is my grief, my mortification, my resentment.—A fine army destroyed, our invaluable officers slain, the cause of Europe lost, and all by insincerity and treason! The Spaniards knew our friendship, they saw our successes, and they introduced us into a desert to leave us to perish! Even victory, that victory which cost us our commander, while it restored to us our rifled honour, and gave us the power of returning home as became free-born Britons, could not reawaken the dead, could not revive the expiring soldiers whom Spanish deceit, by exposing them to want and unmentionable miseries, had even murdered.

Here we have landed upwards, of two thousand sick. Very few of them are wounded: it was not the battle, but the march which reduced them to this condition. None are allowed to come on shore but the actually ill; I wish our orders were different; for, in the case of the wind remaining for any time adverse, the hand of contagion will. supersede these commands, and send the men who are probably well, full of infection into the hospitals of Plymouth. A few days on shore to disengage themselves from the noisome effects of a Spanish campaign and to inhale renewed health in the fresh breezes of the land, would probably have preserved many a brave man alive who now lies discontented and sickening within the pestilential decks of the transports.

Indeed, I fear, go on shore when they will, that unless some efficient means are taken to prepare their famished stomachs to take in food by degrees, the climax of these poor men's miseries is not yet completed. Should they eat and drink as their exhausted frames will excite them, the most serious consequences may be dreaded, and hundreds, if not thousands, may fall the victims.

Probably you will accuse me of gloom; and that I have lately learnt a sad propensity to evil anticipations; but consider my situation; when I see death on all sides of me, how can I help knowing what immediately leads to its dismal confines? Since I have been these few days in harbour, the numbers we have buried are incalculable. Our officers are dropping off hourly; and the mixture of joy, grief, and pity, shewn by the kind inhabitants to the invalids, the dying, and those who live to lament their friends, excites our gratitude and admiration.

They receive the sick officers into their houses, entertaining and cherishing them with the hospitality of friends and the tenderness of relations. The soldiers too share these kindnesses. Private carriages are sent down to the landing places to convey the invalid men to the hospitals; and, when there, a thousand little comforts are sent to them by various good families in the town.

You can imagine how glad these wretched fellow sufferers must be of being so determinately ill as to make it necessary to take them out of the transports, when I tell you that in the vessel which brought me over were three hundred souls, besides thirteen officers. We, of the latter unlucky number, were all thrust together into one filthy little cabin, with no other beds than those hard ones we had long been used to; namely, the floor, and a blanket with which we enveloped our haggard persons.

I know not, now that I have again tasted the sweets of cleanliness, how I shall be able to endure a second imprisonment in that cell of nastiness; but necessity has no law, and as it is our duty to be resigned to what is inevitable, you shall hear that I have suffered this repetition of purgatory with soldier-like patience.

While I am yet bird-limed to these vessels, I must not omit acquainting you with a few particulars which I learnt while on board, relative to the affair at Beneventè, when General Le Febre was made prisoner. Several dragoons belonging to the different detachments that fought on that day claim the honour of taking this officer. In our transport we had some of the Third German Light Dragoons.

One of the men, an exceedingly fine fellow, told me that he was the fortunate hero. His account is, that during the action he saw a French officer on full speed crossing the plain, as if making towards the river: he instantly pursued, and gaining upon him, General Le Febre (for it was he) turned round, and laying one of his pistols deliberately on his bridle-arm to take the surer aim, he fired. But on its not taking effect upon his pursuer, and finding that he should soon be closed with, and judging of his adversary by what he had seen of his steadiness, he preferred peace to a British *coup de sabre*, and pulling up, surrendered. As a trophy of his conquest, the soldier now possesses the embroidered belt and *cartouch*-box of his prisoner.

General Stewart came up almost at this juncture. He received the French commander from the dragoon, and paying him many deserved encomiums on his gallantry, promised that it should not go unrewarded. I have no doubt that the English general will perform his word, as no feeling can be more delightful to the heart of a brave man, than the emotions which accompany the rewarding of brave acts in others.

We few convalescents are overwhelmed with questions relative to our sufferings and our lasses. I regret that my answers are even more dismal than the expectations of the interrogators. The two questions most frequently asked me are, "how many persons we have lost, dead by fatigue and the battle; and how many are taken prisoners: and what number of horses were destroyed?"

To the first demand I can only make a vague guess; but yet, I think it is pretty near the mark, at least it is within it, the subject being too full of distress to admit exaggeration. Taking in the whole of our loss from the time of General Moore's march from Lisbon to our embarkation at Corunna, I should think we might say that we have been deprived of between 7000 and

8000 men; as to the number of horses we have lost, I cannot pretend to enumerate them. Our mules were all destroyed; and for the dragoon horses, I fear that out of so glorious a body, not more than eighty or ninety were preserved alive in each regiment.

As the greater number of these invaluable animals were lost by a want of active military experience on our part, I hope that our cavalry officers, having received so severe a lesson in our late campaign, will in future guard against similar errors. In the field they were all that a soldier could wish; both officer and horse were then in their right element; and no sight could be grander than our embattled squadrons making the charge with a steadiness and force that bore down all before them. The French officers not only acknowledged the superiority of our cavalry over theirs, but declared them to be the finest in the world.

With such troops, and with an infantry worthy to support them, had we been but honestly treated in Spain, what might we not have effected! Having seen the means of immortal glory wasted; having beheld streams of blood flowing in vain; enduring the loss of all that is dear to a soldier, excepting his honour; the reflections which rise to my mind are too poignant to be borne, I cannot bear to think on it.

All that I can say under these grievous remembrances, when I hear even now that another expedition is intended for Spain, is this: —that I hope it will be supported with more sincerity than we experienced; and that before it ventures on those deceptive shores, that our leaders at home will not suffer themselves to be again betrayed by traitors affecting patriotism, and whose artifices seek to serve the enemy by weakening Great Britain.

One of the French officers, our prisoner, said to me during our retreat: "Your country and your general little know how nearly your army was becoming ours by purchase."

I answered, "No Englishman would thus sell his honour."

"No, your Spanish friends."

It instantly struck me that Morla, who sold his conscience and the capital, and with that his country, was to have drawn us also into the snare! How ought we to thank the memory of our commander that we were not thus made a prey!

Adieu! The moment I land at Portsmouth you shall see your friend.

P.S. I enclose the route of our army during this disastrous campaign.

March of the army under the command of Lieutenant-General Sir John Moore, from Lisbon to Salamanca, through Portugal, naming the principal towns they passed through.

Lisbon.

Santiram.

Abrantes.

Castello Branco.

Guarda.

Almeida.

Ciudad Rodriga.

Salamanca.

General Hope's division.

Lisbon, crossed the Tagus to:—

Aldea Golego.

Estremoz.

Elvas.

Badajos.

Truxillo.

Guadaloupe.

Toledo.

Madrid

Escurial.

Avila.

Alva.——Salamanca.

The junction being now formed of our columns, we proceeded to—

Toro.

Valdaris.

Majorga,—Here joined by General Baird's force from Corunna.

Sahagun, back to:—

Majorga.

Benevente.

Astorga.

Villa Franca.

Lugo.

Betanzas

Corunna.

LEONAUR

ALSO FROM LEONAUR

AVAILABLE IN SOFTCOVER OR HARDCOVER WITH DUST JACKET

A HISTORY OF THE FRENCH & INDIAN WAR *by Arthur G. Bradley*—The Seven Years War as it was fought in the New World has always fascinated students of military history—here is the story of that confrontation.

WASHINGTON'S EARLY CAMPAIGNS *by James Hadden*—The French Post Expedition, Great Meadows and Braddock's Defeat—including Braddock's Orderly Books.

BOUQUET & THE OHIO INDIAN WAR *by Cyrus Cort & William Smith*—Two Accounts of the Campaigns of 1763-1764: Bouquet's Campaigns by Cyrus Cort & The History of Bouquet's Expeditions by William Smith.

NARRATIVES OF THE FRENCH & INDIAN WAR: 2 *by David Holden, Samuel Jenks, Lemuel Lyon, Mary Cochrane Rogers & Henry T. Blake*—Contains The Diary of Sergeant David Holden, Captain Samuel Jenks' Journal, The Journal of Lemuel Lyon, Journal of a French Officer at the Siege of Quebec, A Battle Fought on Snowshoes & The Battle of Lake George.

NARRATIVES OF THE FRENCH & INDIAN WAR *by Brown, Eastburn, Hawks & Putnam*—Ranger Brown's Narrative, The Adventures of Robert Eastburn, The Journal of Rufus Putnam—Provincial Infantry & Orderly Book and Journal of Major John Hawks on the Ticonderoga-Crown Point Campaign.

THE 7TH (QUEEN'S OWN) HUSSARS: Volume 1—1688-1792 *by C. R. B. Barrett*—As Dragoons During the Flanders Campaign, War of the Austrian Succession and the Seven Years War.

INDIA'S FREE LANCES *by H. G. Keene*—European Mercenary Commanders in Hindustan 1770-1820.

THE BENGAL EUROPEAN REGIMENT *by P. R. Innes*—An Elite Regiment of the Honourable East India Company 1756-1858.

MUSKET & TOMAHAWK *by Francis Parkman*—A Military History of the French & Indian War, 1753-1760.

THE BLACK WATCH AT TICONDEROGA *by Frederick B. Richards*—Campaigns in the French & Indian War.

QUEEN'S RANGERS *by Frederick B. Richards*—John Simcoe and his Rangers During the Revolutionary War for America.

www.ingramcontent.com/pod-product-compliance
Lightning Source LLC
Chambersburg PA
CBHW021111090426
42738CB00006B/594